Capital Budgeting:
Theory and Practice

The Frank J. Fabozzi Series

Fixed Income Securities, Second Edition by Frank J. Fabozzi

Focus on Value: A Corporate and Investor Guide to Wealth Creation by James L. Grant and James A. Abate

The Handbook of Global Fixed Income Calculations by Dragomir Krgin

Real Options and Option-Embedded Securities by William T. Moore

Managing a Corporate Bond Portfolio by Leland E. Crabbe and Frank J. Fabozzi

Capital Budgeting: Theory and Practice

Pamela P. Peterson, Ph.D., CFA

Frank J. Fabozzi, Ph.D., CFA

JOHN WILEY & SONS

Published by John Wiley & Sons, Inc.
Published simultaneously in Canada.

ISBN: 0-471-21833-2

10 9 8 7 6 5 4 3 2 1

PPP

To my kids, Erica and Ken

FJF

To my wife, Donna,
and my children, Karly, Patricia, and Francesco

About the Authors

Pamela P. Peterson, PhD, CFA is a professor of finance at Florida State University where she teaches undergraduate courses in corporate finance and doctoral courses in empirical research methods. Professor Peterson has published articles in journals including the *Journal of Finance*, the *Journal of Financial Economics*, the *Journal of Banking and Finance*, *Financial Management*, and the *Financial Analysts Journal*. She is the coauthor of *Analysis of Financial Statements*, published by Frank J. Fabozzi Associates, author of *Financial Management and Analysis*, published by McGraw-Hill, and co-author with David R. Peterson of the AIMR monograph *Company Performance and Measures of Value Added.*

Frank J. Fabozzi is editor of the *Journal of Portfolio Management* and an adjunct professor of finance at Yale University's School of Management. He is a Chartered Financial Analyst and Certified Public Accountant. Dr. Fabozzi is on the board of directors of the Guardian Life family of funds and the BlackRock complex of funds. He earned a doctorate in economics from the City University of New York in 1972 and in 1994 received an honorary doctorate of Humane Letters from Nova Southeastern University. Dr. Fabozzi is a Fellow of the International Center for Finance at Yale University.

Preface

Corporate financial managers continually invest funds in assets, and these assets produce income and cash flows that the firm can then either reinvest in more assets or distribute to the owners of the firm. Capital investment refers to the firm's investment in assets, and these investments may be either short term or long term in nature. Capital budgeting decisions involve the long-term commitment of a firm's scarce resources in capital investments. When such a decision is made, the firm is committed to a current and possibly future outlay of funds.

Capital budgeting decisions play a prominent role in determining whether a firm will be successful. The commitment of funds to a particular capital project can be enormous and may be irreversible. While some capital budgeting decisions are routine decisions that do not change the course or risk of a firm, there are strategic capital budgeting decisions that will either have an effect on the firm's future market position in its current product lines or permit it to expand into new product lines in the future. The annals of business history are replete with examples of how capital budgeting decisions turned the tide for a company. For example, the producer of photographic copying paper, the Haloid Corporation, made a decision to commit a substantial portion of its capital to the development of xerography. How important was that decision? Well, in 1958, the Haloid Corporation changes its name to Haloid-Xerox. In 1961 it became Xerox.

In *Capital Budgeting: Theory and Practice*, we discuss and illustrate the different aspects of the capital budgeting decision process. In Section I we discuss the capital budgeting decision and cash flows. In Chapter 1 we explain the investment problem. In that chapter we describe the five stages in the capital budgeting process—investment screening and selection, capital budgeting proposal, budgeting approval and authorization, project tracking, and postcompletion audit—and the classification of investment projects—according to their economic life, according to their risk, and according to their dependence on other projects. We discuss the critical task of cash flow estimation in Chapter 2 and offer two hypothetical examples to illustrate cash flow estimation in Chapter 3.

In Section II, we cover the techniques for evaluating capital budgeting proposals and for selecting projects. We explain each technique in terms of the maximization of owners' wealth and how each technique deals with the following: (1) Does the technique consider all cash flows from the project? (2) Does the technique consider the timing of cash flows? and (3) Does the technique consider the riskiness of cash flows? The techniques covered include the payback and discounted payback, net present value, profitability index, internal rate of return, and modified internal rate of return. In Chapter 9 we conclude Section II with a discussion of several issues: scale differences (including capital rationing), choosing the appropriate technique, capital budgeting in practice (including conflicts with responsibility center performance evaluation measures), and the justification of new technology.

Capital budgeting projects typically involve risk. In Section III we explain how to incorporate risk into the capital budgeting decision. This involves considering the following factors: future cash flows, the degree of uncertainty of these cash flows, and the value of these cash flows given the level of uncertainty about realizing them. In Chapter 10 we cover the measurement of project risk—measuring a project's stand-alone risk, sensitivity analysis, simulation analysis, and measuring a project's market risk. In Chapter 11, we demonstrate how to incorporate risk into the capital budgeting process by adjusting the discount rate, describe how a project can be evaluated using certainty equivalents, and then discuss the treatment of risk using real options. The real option approach applies the well-developed theory of options pricing to capital budgeting.

In the last section, we explain a common capital budgeting decision: the decision to buy an asset with borrowed funds or lease the same asset. This is the "lease versus borrow-to-buy decision." A key factor in the analysis is the ability of the firm to use the tax benefits associated with ownership of an asset—depreciation and tax credits, if any. Several models have been proposed to assess whether to buy or lease. A model to value a lease for a firm that is in a current taxpaying position is explained in Chapter 12. In Chapter 13 we explain how uncertainty is incorporated into the lease valuation model. The model explained in Chapter 12 is generalized in Chapter

14 to cases where the firm is currently in a nontaxpaying position but expects to resume paying taxes at some specified future date. We provide the fundamentals of leasing in the appendix to the book.

Pamela P. Peterson
Frank J. Fabozzi

Contents

Section I

Making Investment Decisions

The value of a particular asset isn't always easy to determine. However, managers are continually faced with decisions about which assets to invest in. In this chapter, we will look at the different types of investment decisions the financial manager faces. We will also discuss ways to estimate the benefits and costs associated with these decisions.

The financial manager's objective is to maximize owners' wealth. To accomplish this, the manager must evaluate investment opportunities and determine which ones will add value to the firm. For example, consider three firms, Firms A, B, and C, each having identical assets and investment opportunities, except that:

- Firm A's management does not take advantage of its investment opportunities and simply pays all of its earnings to its owners;
- Firm B's management only makes those investments necessary to replace deteriorating plant and equipment, paying out any left-over earnings to its owners; and
- Firm C's management invests in all those opportunities that provide a return better than what the owners could have earned if they had invested the funds themselves.

In the case of Firm A, the owners' investment in the firm will not be as profitable as it would be if the firm had taken advantage of better investment opportunities. By failing to invest even to replace deteriorating plant and equipment, Firm A will eventually shrink until it has no more assets. Firm B's management is not taking advantage of all profitable investments. This means that there are forgone opportunities, and owners' wealth is not maximized. But Firm C's management is making all profitable investments and thus maximizing owners' wealth. Firm C will continue to grow as long as there are profitable investment opportunities and as long as its management takes advantage of them.

In Chapter 1, we will describe the process of making investment decisions. We will look at estimating how much a firm's cash flows will change in the future as a result of an investment decision. The main topic of Chapter 2, estimating cash flow, is an imprecise art at best. Therefore, after we describe in detail a method for estimating cash flows in Chapter 2. In Chapter 3 we provide two integrative examples. We conclude Chapter 3 with an explanation of some ways in which managers sometimes deviate from our ideal method in actual practice.

In Section II, we will analyze the change in the firm's cash flows using techniques that lead the financial manager to a decision regarding whether to invest in a project. In Section III, we see how uncertainty affects the cost of capital and, hence, the investment decision.

Chapter 1

The Investment Problem and Capital Budgeting

Firms continually invest funds in assets, and these assets produce income and cash flows that the firm can then either reinvest in more assets or pay to the owners. These assets represent the firm's capital. *Capital* is the firm's total assets. It includes all tangible and intangible assets. These assets include physical assets (such as land, buildings, equipment, and machinery), as well as assets that represent property rights (such as accounts receivable, securities, patents, and copyrights). When we refer to *capital investment*, we are referring to the firm's investment in its assets.

The term "capital" also has come to mean the funds used to finance the firm's assets. In this sense, capital consists of notes, bonds, stock, and short-term financing. We use the term "capital structure" to refer to the mix of these different sources of capital used to finance a firm's assets.

The firm's capital investment decision may be comprised of a number of distinct decisions, each referred to as a *project*. A *capital project* is a set of assets that are contingent on one another and are considered together. For example, suppose a firm is considering the production of a new product. This capital project would require the firm to acquire land, build facilities, and purchase production equipment. And this project may also require the firm to increase its investment in its *working capital* — inventory, cash, or accounts receivable. Working capital is the collection of assets needed for day-to-day operations that support a firm's long-term investments.

The investment decisions of the firm are decisions concerning a firm's capital investment. When we refer to a particular decision that financial managers must make, we are referring to a decision pertaining to a capital project.

INVESTMENT DECISIONS AND
OWNERS' WEALTH MAXIMIZATION

Managers must evaluate a number of factors in making investment decisions. Not only does the financial manager need to estimate how much the firm's future cash flows will change if it invests in a project, but the manager must also evaluate the uncertainty associated with these future cash flows.

We already know that the value of the firm today is the present value of all its future cash flows. But we need to understand better where these future cash flows come from. They come from:

- Assets that are already in place, which are the assets accumulated as a result of all past investment decisions, and
- Future investment opportunities

The value of the firm, is therefore,

Value of firm = Present value of all future cash flows
　　　　　 = Present value of cash flows from all assets in place
　　　　　 + Present value of cash flows from future investment opportunities

Future cash flows are discounted at a rate that represents investors' assessments of the uncertainty that these cash flows will flow in the amounts and when expected. To evaluate the value of the firm, we need to evaluate the risk of these future cash flows.

Cash flow risk comes from two basic sources:

- *Sales risk*, which is the degree of uncertainty related to the number of units that will be sold and the price of the good or service; and
- *Operating risk*, which is the degree of uncertainty concerning operating cash flows that arises from the particular mix of fixed and variable operating costs

Sales risk is related to the economy and the market in which the firm's goods and services are sold. Operating risk, for the most part, is determined by the product or service that the firm provides and is related to the sensitivity of operating cash flows to changes in sales. We refer to the combination of these two risks as *business risk*.

A project's business risk is reflected in the discount rate, which is the rate of return required to compensate the suppliers of capital (bondholders and owners) for the amount of risk they bear. From the perspective of investors, the discount rate is the *required rate of return* (RRR). From the firm's perspective, the discount rate is the *cost of capital* — what it costs the firm to raise a dollar of new capital.

For example, suppose a firm invests in a new project. How does the investment affect the firm's value? If the project generates cash flows that *just* compensate the suppliers of capital for the risk they bear on this project (that is, it earns the cost of capital), the value of the firm does not change. If the project generates cash flows *greater* than needed to compensate them for the risk they take on, it earns more than the cost of capital, increasing the value of the firm. If the project generates cash flows *less* than needed, it earns less than the cost of capital, decreasing the value of the firm.

How do we know whether the cash flows are more than or less than needed to compensate for the risk that they will indeed need? If we discount all the cash flows at the cost of capital, we can assess how this project affects the present value of the firm. If the expected change in the value of the firm from an investment is:

- positive, the project returns more than the cost of capital;
- negative, the project returns less than the cost of capital;
- zero, the project returns the cost of capital.

Capital budgeting is the process of identifying and selecting investments in long-lived assets, or assets expected to produce benefits over more than one year. In Section II, we discuss how to evaluate cash flows in deciding whether or not to invest. We cover how to determine cash flow risk and factor this risk into capital budgeting decisions in Section III.

CAPITAL BUDGETING

Because a firm must continually evaluate possible investments, capital budgeting is an ongoing process. However, before a firm begins thinking about capital budgeting, it must first determine its *corporate strategy* — its broad set of objectives for future investment. For example, the Walt Disney Company's objective is to "be the world's premier family entertainment company through the ongoing development of its powerful brand and character franchises."[1]

Consider the corporate strategy of Mattel, Inc., manufacturer of toys such as Barbie and Disney toys. Mattel's strategy is to become a full-line toy company and grow through expansion into the international toy market. In the early 1990's, Mattel entered into the activity toy, games, and plush toy markets, and, through acquisitions in Mexico, France, and Japan, increased its presence in the international toy market.[2]

How does a firm achieve its corporate strategy? By making investments in long-lived assets that will maximize owners' wealth. Selecting these projects is what capital budgeting is all about.

Stages in the Capital Budgeting Process

There are five stages in the capital budgeting process.

Stage 1: *Investment screening and selection*

Projects consistent with the corporate strategy are identified by production, marketing, and research and development management of the firm. Once identified, projects are evaluated and screened by estimating how they affect the future cash flows of the firm and, hence, the value of the firm.

Stage 2: *Capital budget proposal*

A capital budget is proposed for the projects surviving the screening and selection process. The budget lists the recommended projects and the dollar amount of investment needed for each. This proposal may start as an estimate of expected revenues and costs, but as the project analysis is refined, data from marketing, purchasing, engineering, accounting, and finance functions are put together.

---

[1] *The Walt Disney Company Annual Report 2000*: 10.
[2] *Mattel, Inc., 1991 Annual Report*: 4–5, 15.

Stage 3: *Budgeting approval and authorization*
Projects included in the capital budget are authorized, allowing further fact gathering and analysis, and approved, allowing expenditures for the projects. In some firms, the projects are authorized and approved at the same time. In others, a project must first be authorized, requiring more research before it can be formally approved. Formal authorization and approval procedures are typically used on larger expenditures; smaller expenditures are at the discretion of management.

Stage 4: *Project tracking*
After a project is approved, work on it begins. The manager reports periodically on its expenditures, as well as on any revenues associated with it. This is referred to as *project tracking*, the communication link between the decision makers and the operating management of the firm. For example: tracking can identify cost over-runs and uncover the need for more marketing research.

Stage 5: *Postcompletion audit*
Following a period of time, perhaps two or three years after approval, projects are reviewed to see whether they should be continued. This reevaluation is referred to as a *postcompletion audit*. Thorough postcompletion audits are typically performed on selected projects, usually the largest projects in a given year's budget for the firm or for each division. Postcompletion audits show the firm's management how well the cash flows realized correspond with the cash flows forecasted several years earlier.

Classifying Investment Projects

In this section, we discuss different ways managers classify capital investment projects. One way of classifying projects is by project life, whether short-term or long-term. We do this because in the case of long-term projects, the time value of money plays an important role in long-term projects. Another ways of classifying projects is by their risk. The riskier the project's future cash flows, the greater the role of the cost of capital in decision-making. Still another way of classifying projects is by their dependence on other projects. The relationship between a project's cash flows and the cash flows of some other project of the firm must be incorporated explicitly into the analysis since we want to analyze how a project affects the total cash flows of the firm.

Classification According to Their Economic Life

An investment generally provides benefits over a limited period of time, referred to as its economic life. The *economic life* or *useful life* of an asset is determined by:

- physical deterioration;
- obsolescence; or
- the degree of competition in the market for a product.

The economic life is an estimate of the length of time that the asset will provide benefits to the firm. After its useful life, the revenues generated by the asset tend to decline rapidly and its expenses tend to increase.

Typically, an investment requires an immediate expenditure and provides benefits in the form of cash flows received in the future. If benefits are received only within the current period — within one year of making the investment — we refer to the investment as a *short-term investment*. If these benefits are received beyond the current period, we refer to the investment as a *long-term investment* and refer to the expenditure as a *capital expenditure*. An investment project may comprise one or more capital expenditures. For example, a new product may require investment in production equipment, a building, and transportation equipment.

Short-term investment decisions involve, primarily, investments in current assets: cash, marketable securities, accounts receivable, and inventory. The objective of investing in short-term assets is the same as long-term assets: maximizing owners' wealth. Nevertheless, we consider them separately for two practical reasons:

1. Decisions about long-term assets are based on projections of

cash flows far into the future and require us to consider the time value of money.

2. Long-term assets do not figure into the daily operating needs of the firm.

Decisions regarding short-term investments, or current assets, are concerned with day-to-day operations. And a firm needs some level of current assets to act as a cushion in case of unusually poor operating periods, when cash flows from operations are less than expected.

Classification According to Their Risk

Suppose you are faced with two investments, A and B, each promising a $100 cash inflow ten years from today. If A is riskier than B, what are they worth to you today? If you do not like risk, you would consider A less valuable than B because the chance of getting the $100 in ten years is less for A than for B. Therefore, valuing a project requires considering the risk associated with its future cash flows.

The investment's risk of return can be classified according to the nature of the project represented by the investment:

- *Replacement projects:* investments in the replacement of existing equipment or facilities
- *Expansion projects:* investments in projects that broaden existing product lines and existing markets
- *New products and markets:* projects that involve introducing a new product or entering into a new market
- *Mandated projects:* projects required by government laws or agency rules

Replacement projects include the maintenance of existing assets to continue the current level of operating activity. Projects that reduce costs, such as replacing old equipment or improving the efficiency, are also considered replacement projects. To evaluate replacement projects we need to compare the value of the firm with the replacement asset to the value of the firm without that same replacement asset. What we're really doing in this comparison is looking at *opportunity costs*: what cash flows would have been if the firm had stayed with the old asset.

There's little risk in the cash flows from replacement projects. The firm is simply replacing equipment or buildings already operating and producing cash flows. And the firm typically has experience in managing similar new equipment.

Expansion projects, which are intended to enlarge a firm's established product or market, also involve little risk. However, investment projects that involve introducing new products or entering into new markets are riskier because the firm has little or no management experience in the new product or market.

A firm is forced or coerced into its mandated projects. These are government-mandated projects typically found in "heavy" industries, such as utilities, transportation, and chemicals, all industries requiring a large portion of their assets in production activities. Government agencies, such as the Occupational Health and Safety Agency (OSHA) or the Environmental Protection Agency (EPA), may impose requirements that firms install specific equipment or alter their activities (such as how they dispose of waste).

We can further classify mandated projects into two types: contingent and retroactive. Suppose, as a steel manufacturer, we are required by law to include pollution control devices on all smoke stacks. If we are considering a new plant, this mandated equipment is really part of our new plant investment decision — the investment in pollution control equipment is contingent on our building the new plant.

On the other hand, if we are required by law to place pollution control devices on existing smoke stacks, the law is retroactive. We do not have a choice. We must invest in the equipment whether it increases the value of the firm or not. In this case, either select from among possible equipment that satisfies the mandate or we weigh the decision whether to halt production in the offending plant.

Classification According to Their Dependence on Other Projects

In addition to considering the future cash flows generated by a project, a firm must consider how it affects the assets already in place — the results of previous project decisions — as well as other projects that may be undertaken. Projects can be classified according to the degree of dependence with other projects: independent projects, mutually exclusive projects, contingent projects, and complementary projects.

An *independent project* is one whose cash flows are not related to the cash flows of any other project. Accepting or rejecting an independent project does not affect the acceptance or rejection of other projects. Projects are *mutually exclusive* if the acceptance of one precludes the acceptance of other projects. For example, suppose a manufacturer is considering whether to replace its production facilities with more modern equipment. The firm may solicit bids among the different manufacturers of this equipment. The decision consists of comparing two choices, either keeping its existing production facilities or replacing the facilities with the modern equipment of one manufacturer. Since the firm cannot use more than one production facility, it must evaluate each bid and choose the most attractive one. The alternative production facilities are mutually exclusive projects: the firm can accept only one bid.

Contingent projects are dependent on the acceptance of another project. Suppose a greeting card company develops a new character, Pippy, and is considering starting a line of Pippy cards. If Pippy catches on, the firm will consider producing a line of Pippy T-shirts — but *only* if the Pippy character becomes popular. The T-shirt project is a contingent project.

Another form of dependence is found in *complementary projects*, where the investment in one enhances the cash flows of one or more other projects. Consider a manufacturer of personal computer equipment and software. If it develops new software that enhances the abilities of a computer mouse, the introduction of this new software may enhance its mouse sales as well.

Chapter 2

Cash Flow Estimation

A firm invests only to increase the value of their ownership interest. A firm will have cash flows in the future from its past investment decisions. When it invests in new assets, it expects the future cash flows to be *greater than without this new investment*.

INCREMENTAL CASH FLOWS

The difference between the cash flows of the firm *with* the investment project and the cash flows of the firm *without* the investment project — both over the same period of time — is referred to as the project's *incremental cash flows*.

To evaluate an investment, we'll have to look at how it will change the future cash flows of the firm. We will be examining how much the value of the firm changes as a result of the investment.

The change in a firm's value as a result of a new investment is the difference between its benefits and its costs:

Project's change in the value of the firm
= Project's benefits − Project's costs

A more useful way of evaluating the change in the value is the breakdown of the project's cash flows into two components:

1. The present value of the cash flows from the project's operating activities (revenues minus operating expenses), referred to as the project's *operating cash flows* (OCF); and
2. The present value of the *investment cash flows*, which are the expenditures needed to acquire the project's assets and any cash flows from disposing the project's assets.

Or,

Change in the value of the firm
= Present value of the change in operating cash flows
provided by the project
+ Present value of investment cash flows

The present value of a project's operating cash flows is typically positive (indicating predominantly cash inflows) and the present value of the investment cash flows is typically negative (indicating predominantly cash outflows).

INVESTMENT CASH FLOWS

When we consider the cash flows of an investment, we must also consider all the cash flows associated with acquiring and disposing of assets in the investment. Let's first become familiar with cash flows related to acquiring assets; then we'll look at cash flows related to disposing of assets.

Asset Acquisition

In acquiring any asset, there are three cash flows to consider:

1. Cost of the asset
2. Set-up expenditures, including shipping and installation
3. Any tax credit

The tax credit may be an investment tax credit or a special credit — such as a credit for a pollution control device — depending on the prevailing tax law.

The cash flow associated with acquiring an asset is:

Cash flow from acquiring assets
= Cost + Set-up expenditures − Tax credit

Suppose the firm buys equipment that costs $100,000 and it costs $10,000 to install it. If the firm is eligible for a 10% tax credit on this equipment (that is, 10% of the total cost of buying and installing the equipment), the change in the firm's cash flow from acquiring the asset of $99,000 is:

Cash flow from acquiring assets
$$= \$100,000 + \$10,000 - 0.10(\$100,000 + \$10,000)$$
$$= \$100,000 + \$10,000 - \$11,000 = \$99,000$$

The cash outflow is $99,000 when this asset is acquired: $110,000 *out* to buy and install the equipment and $11,000 *in* from the reduction in taxes.

What about expenditures made in the past for assets or research that would be used in the project we're evaluating? Suppose the firm spent $1,000,000 over the past three years developing a new type of toothpaste. Should the firm consider this $1,000,000 spent on research and development when deciding whether to produce this new project we are considering? No: these expenses have already been made and do not affect how the new product changes the future cash flows of the firm. We refer to this $1,000,000 as a *sunk cost* and do not consider it in the analysis of our new project. Whether or not the firm goes ahead with this new product, this $1,000,000 has been spent. A sunk cost is any cost that has already been incurred that does not affect future cash flows of the firm.

Let's consider another example. Suppose the firm owns a building that is currently empty. Let's say the firm suddenly has an opportunity to use it for the production of a new product. Is the cost of the building relevant to the new product decision? The cost of the building itself is a sunk cost since it was an expenditure made as part of some *previous* investment decision. The cost of the building does not affect the decision to go ahead with the new product.

Suppose the firm was using the building in some way producing cash (say, renting it) and the new project is going to take over the entire building. The cash flows given up represent opportunity costs that must be included in the analysis of the new project. However, these forgone cash flows are not asset acquisition cash flows. Because they represent operating cash flows that could have occurred but will not because of the new project, they must be considered part of the project's future operating cash flows.

Further, if we incur costs in renovating the building to manufacture the new product, the renovation costs are relevant and should be included in our asset acquisition cash flows.[1]

Asset Disposition

At the end of the useful life of an asset, the firm may be able to sell it or may have to pay someone to haul it away. If the firm is making a decision that involves replacing an existing asset, the cash flow from disposing of the old asset must be figured in since it is a cash flow relevant to the acquisition of the new asset.

If the firm disposes of an asset, whether at the end of its useful life or when it is replaced, two types of cash flows must be considered:

1. what you receive or pay in disposing of the asset
2. any tax consequences resulting from the disposal

Cash flow from disposing assets
= Proceeds or payment from disposing assets
− Taxes from disposing assets

The proceeds are what you expect to sell the asset for, if you can get someone to buy it. If the firm must pay for the disposal of the asset, this cost is a cash outflow.

Consider the investment in a gas station. The current owner wants to sell the station to another gas station proprietor. But if a buyer cannot be found and the station is abandoned, the current owner may be required to remove the underground gasoline storage tanks to prevent environmental damage. Thus, a cost is incurred at the end of the asset's life.

The tax consequences are a bit more complicated. Taxes depend on: (1) the expected sales price, (2) the book value of the asset for tax purposes at the time of disposition, and (3) the tax rate at the time of disposal.

If a firm sells the asset for more than its book value but less than its original cost, the difference between the sales price and the book value for tax purposes (called the *tax basis*) is a gain, taxable

---

[1] This assumes, of course, that the firm would not be using or selling this building.

at ordinary tax rates. If a firm sells the asset for more than its original cost, then the gain is broken into two parts:

1. *Capital gain:* the difference between the sales price and the original cost
2. *Recapture of depreciation:* the difference between the original cost and the tax basis

The *capital gain* is the benefit from the appreciation in the value of the asset and may be taxed at special rates, depending on the tax law at the time of sale. The *recapture of depreciation* represents the amount by which the firm has *over*depreciated the asset during its life. This means that more depreciation has been deducted from income (reducing taxes) than necessary to reflect the usage of the asset. The recapture portion is taxed at the ordinary tax rates, since this excess depreciation taken all these years has reduced taxable income.

If a firm sells an asset for less than its book value, the result is a *capital loss*. In this case, the asset's value has decreased by more than the amount taken for depreciation for tax purposes. A capital loss is given special tax treatment:

- If there are capital gains in the same tax year as the capital loss, they are combined, so that the capital loss reduces the taxes paid on capital gains, and
- If there are no capital gains to offset against the capital loss, the capital loss is used to reduce ordinary taxable income.

The benefit from a loss on the sale of an asset is the amount by which taxes are reduced. The reduction in taxable income is referred to as a *tax-shield*, since the loss *shields* some income from taxation. If the firm has a loss of $1,000 on the sale of an asset and has a tax rate of 40%, this means that its taxable income is $1,000 less and its taxes are $400 less than they would have been without the sale of the asset.

Suppose you are evaluating an asset that costs $10,000 that you expect to sell in five years. Suppose further that the tax basis of the asset for tax purposes will be $3,000 after five years and that the firm's tax rate is 40%. What are the expected cash flows from disposing this asset?

If the firm expects to sell the asset for $8,000 in five years, $10,000 − $3,000 = $7,000 of the asset's cost will be depreciated; yet the asset lost only $10,000 − $8,000 = $2,000 in value. Therefore, the firm has overdepreciated the asset by $5,000. Since this overdepreciation represents deductions to be taken on the firm's tax returns over the five years that don't reflect the actual depreciation in value (the asset doesn't lose $7,000 in value, only $2,000), this $5,000 is taxed at ordinary tax rates. If the firm's tax rate is 40%, the tax will be 40% × $5,000 = $2,000.

The cash flow from disposition is the sum of the direct cash flow (someone pays us for the asset or the firm pays someone to dispose of it) and the tax consequences. In this example, the cash flow is the $8,000 we expect someone to pay the firm for the asset, less the $2,000 in taxes we expect the firm to pay, or $6,000 cash inflow.

Suppose instead that the firm expects to sell this asset in five years for $12,000. Again, the asset is overdepreciated by $7,000. In fact, the asset is not expected to depreciate, but rather *appreciate* over the five years. The $7,000 in depreciation is recaptured after five years and taxed at ordinary rates: 40% of $7,000, or $2,800. The $2,000 capital gain is the appreciation in the value of the asset and may be taxed at special rates. If the tax rate on capital gain income is 30%, you expect the firm to pay 30% of $2,000, or $600 in taxes on this gain. Selling the asset in five years for $12,000 therefore results in an expected cash inflow of $12,000 − $2,800 − $600 = $8,600.

Suppose the firm expects to sell the asset in five years for $1,000. If the firm can reduce its ordinary taxable income by the amount of the capital loss, $3,000 − $1,000 = $2,000, its tax bill will be 40% of $2,000, or $800, because of this loss. We refer to this reduction in the taxes as a *tax-shield*, since the loss "shields" $2,000 of income from taxes. Combining the $800 tax reduction with the cash flow from selling the asset, the $1,000, gives the firm a cash inflow of $1,800.[2]

The calculation of the cash flow from disposition for the alternative sales prices of $8,000, $12,000, and $1,000 are shown in Exhibit 1.

---

[2] If the firm expects other capital gains five years from now, the amount of the tax shield would be less since this loss would be used to first offset any capital gains taxed at 30%. In this case, the expected tax-shield is only 30% of $2,000, or $600, since we must first use the capital loss to reduce any capital gains.

Exhibit 1: Expected Cash Flows from the Disposition of an Asset

The firm pays $10,000 for an asset and expects to dispose it in five years, when the asset has a book value of $3,000. The firm's ordinary tax rate is 40% and the tax rate on capital gains is 30%.

Original cost > Expected sales price > Tax Basis	
Tax on disposition:	
Sales price	$8,000
Tax basis	3,000
Gain	$5,000
Ordinary tax rate	0.40
Tax on recapture	$2,000
Cash flows:	
Proceeds from disposition	$8,000
Less tax on gain	2,000
Cash flow on disposition	$6,000
Expected sales price > Original cost > Tax basis	
Tax on disposition	
Sales price	$12,000
Original cost	10,000
Capital gain	$ 2,000
Capital gains tax rate	0.30
Tax on capital gain	$ 600
Original cost	$10,000
Tax basis	3,000
Gain (recapture)	$ 7,000
Ordinary tax rate	0.40
Tax on recapture	$ 2,800
Cash flows:	
Proceeds from disposition	$12,000
Less tax on capital gain	600
Less tax on recapture	2,800
Cash flow on disposition	$ 8,600
Tax basis > Expected sales price	
Tax-shield on disposition:	
Book value	$3,000
Tax basis	1,000
Loss	$2,000
Ordinary tax rate	0.40
Tax-shield on loss	$ 800
Cash flows:	
Proceeds from disposition	$1,000
Plus tax-shield on loss	800
Cash flow on disposition	$1,800

Let's also not forget about disposing of any existing assets. Suppose the firm bought equipment ten years ago and at that time expected to be able to sell it 15 years later for $10,000. If the firm decides *today* to replace this equipment, it must consider what it is giving up by *not* disposing of an asset *as planned*. If the firm does not replace the equipment today, the firm would continue to depreciate it for five more years and then sell it for $10,000; if the firm replaces the equipment today, it would not have five more years' depreciation on the replaced equipment and it would not have $10,000 in five years (but perhaps some other amount today). This $10,000 in five years, less any taxes, is a foregone cash flow that we must figure into the investment cash flows. Also, the depreciation the firm would have had on the replaced asset must be considered in analyzing the replacement asset's operating cash flows.

Operating Cash Flows

As we saw in the previous section, in the simplest form of investment, there is a cash outflow when the asset is acquired, and there may be either a cash inflow or an outflow at the end of its economic life. In most cases these are not the only cash flows: the investment may result in changes in revenues, expenditures, taxes, and working capital. These are *operating cash flows* since they result directly from the operating activities — the day-to-day activities of the firm.

What we are after here are *estimates* of operating cash flows. We cannot know for certain what these cash flows will be in the future, but we must attempt to estimate them. What is the basis for these estimates? We base them on marketing research, engineering analyses, operations research, analysis of our competitors, and our managerial experience.

Change in Revenues

Suppose you are a financial analyst for a food processor considering a new investment in a line of frozen dinner products. If you introduce a new ready-to-eat dinner product, your marketing research will indicate how much you should expect to sell. But where do these new product sales come from? Some may come from consumers who do not already buy ready-to-eat products. But some sales may come from consumers who choose to buy other types of ready-to-eat product. It would be nice if these consumers are giving up buying our competitors' ready-to-eat dinners. Yet some of them may be giving up buying your company's other ready-to-eat dinner products. So, when you introduce a new product, you are really interested in how it changes the sales of the entire firm (that is, the incremental sales), rather than the sales of the new product alone.

We also need to consider any foregone revenues — opportunity costs — related to an investment. Suppose a firm owns a building currently being rented to another firm. If we are considering terminating that rental agreement so we can use the building for a new project, we need to consider the foregone rent — what we would have earned from the building. Therefore, the revenues from the new project are really only the additional revenues — the revenues from the new project minus the revenue we could have earned from renting the building.

So, when a firm undertakes a new project, the financial managers want to know how it changes the firm's total revenues, not merely the new product's revenues.

Change in Expenses

When a firm takes on a new project, the costs associated with it will change the firm's expenses. If the investment changes the sales of an existing product, the decision maker must estimate the change in unit sales. Based on that estimate, the estimate of the additional costs of producing the additional number of units is derived by consulting with production management. In addition, an estimate of how the product's inventory may change when production and sales of the product change is also needed.

If the investment involves changes in the costs of production, we compare the costs without this investment with the costs with this investment. For example, if the investment is the replacement of an assembly line machine with a more efficient machine, we need to estimate the change in the firm's overall production costs, such as electricity, labor, materials, and management costs.

A new investment may change not only production costs but also operating costs, such as rental payments and administration costs. Changes in operating costs as a result of a new investment must be considered as part of the changes in the firm's expenses.

Increasing cash expenses are cash outflows, and decreasing cash expense are cash inflows.

Change in Taxes

Taxes figure into the operating cash flows in two ways. First, if revenues and expenses change, taxable income and, therefore, taxes change. That means we need to estimate the change in taxable income resulting from the changes in revenues and expenses resulting from a new project to determine the effect of taxes on the firm.

Second, the deduction for depreciation reduces taxes. Depreciation itself is not a cash flow. But depreciation reduces the taxes that must be paid, shielding income from taxation. The tax-shield from depreciation is like a cash inflow.

Suppose a firm is considering a new product that is expected to generate additional sales of $200,000 and increase expenses by $150,000. If the firm's tax rate is 40%, considering only the change in sales and expenses, taxes go up by $50,000 × 40%, or $20,000. This means that the firm is expected to pay $20,000 more in taxes because of the increase in revenues and expenses.

Let's change this around and consider that the product will generate $200,000 in revenues and $250,000 in expenses. Considering only the change in revenues and expenses, if the tax rate is 40%, taxes go *down* by $50,000 × 40%, or $20,000.[3] This means that we reduce our taxes by $20,000, which is like having a cash inflow of $20,000 from taxes.

Now, consider depreciation. When a firm buys an asset that produces income, the tax laws allow it to depreciate the asset, reducing taxable income by a specified percentage of the asset's cost each year. By reducing taxable income, the firm is reducing its taxes. The reduction in taxes is like a cash inflow since it reduces the firm's cash outflow to the government.

---

[3] This loss creates an immediate cash inflow *if* (1) the firm has other income in the same tax year to apply the $50,000 loss against, or (2) the firm has income in prior tax years, so it can carry back this loss and apply for a refund of prior year's taxes. Otherwise, this loss is carried forward to reduce future tax years' income. In this case, this loss is worth less because the benefit from the loss (the reduction in taxable income) is realized in the future, not today.

Suppose a firm has taxable income of $50,000 before depreciation and a flat tax rate of 40%. If the firm is allowed to deduct depreciation of $10,000, how has this changed the taxes it pays?

	Without depreciation	With depreciation
Taxable income	$50,000	$40,000
Tax rate	0.40	0.40
Taxes	$20,000	$16,000

Depreciation *reduces* the firm's tax-related *cash outflow* by $20,000 − $16,000 = $4,000 or, equivalently, by $10,000 × 40% = $4,000. A reduction in an outflow (taxes in this case) is an inflow. We refer to the effect depreciation has on taxes as the *depreciation tax-shield*.

Depreciation itself is not a cash flow. But in determining cash flows, we are concerned with the effect depreciation has on our taxes — and we all know that taxes are a cash outflow. Since depreciation reduces taxable income, depreciation reduces the tax outflow, which amounts to a cash inflow. For tax purposes, firms are permitted to use accelerated depreciation (specifically the rates specified under the Modified Accelerated Cost Recovery System (MACRS)) or straight-line depreciation. An accelerated method is preferred in most situations since it results in larger deductions sooner in the asset's life than using straight-line depreciation. Therefore, accelerated depreciation, if available, is preferable to straight-line, due to the time value of money.

Under the present tax code, assets are depreciated to a zero book value. Salvage value — what we expect the asset to be worth at the end of its life — is not considered in calculating depreciation. So is salvage value totally irrelevant to the analysis? No. Salvage value is our best guess today of what the asset will be worth at the end of its useful life at some time in the future. Salvage value is our estimate of how much we can get when we dispose of the asset. Just remember, you can ignore it to figure depreciation for tax purposes.

Let's look at another depreciation example, this time considering the effects of replacing an asset has on the depreciation tax-shield cash flow. Suppose you are replacing a machine that you bought five years ago for $75,000. You were depreciating this old machine using straight-line depreciation over ten years, or $7,500 depreciation per year. If you replace it with a new machine that costs $50,000 and is depreciated over five years, or $10,000 each year, how does the change in depreciation affect the cash flows if the firm's tax rate is 30%?

We can calculate the effect two ways:

1. We can compare the depreciation and related tax-shield from the old and the new machines. The depreciation tax-shield on the old machine is 30% of $7,500, or $2,250. The depreciation tax-shield on the new machine is 30% of $10,000, or $3,000. Therefore, the change in the cash flow from depreciation is $3,000 − $2,250 = $750.
2. We can calculate the change in depreciation and calculate the tax-shield related to the change in depreciation. The change in depreciation is $10,000 − 7,500 = $2,500. The change in the depreciation tax-shield is 30% of $2,500, or $750.

Let's look at another example. Suppose a firm invests $50,000 in an asset. And suppose the firm has a choice of depreciating the asset using either:

- an accelerated method over four years, with the rates of 33.33%, 44.45%, 14.81%, and 7.41%, respectively, where these depreciation rates are a percentage of the original cost of the asset; or
- the straight-line method over four years.

If the firm's tax rate is 40% and the cost of capital is 10%, what is the present value of the difference in the cash flows from the depreciation tax-shield each year? It is $796, as shown below:

Year	Depreciation using the accelerated method	Depreciation using the straight-line method	Difference in depreciation	Difference in depreciation tax-shield	Present value of difference
First	$16,665	$12,500	$4,165	$1,666	$1,515
Second	22,225	12,500	9,725	3,890	3,215
Third	7,405	12,500	−5,095	−2,038	−1,531
Fourth	3,705	12,500	−8,795	−3,518	−2,403
	$50,000	$50,000	$0	$0	$796

Using both the accelerated and straight-line methods, the entire asset's cost is depreciated over the four years. But the accelerated method provides greater tax-shields in the first and second years than the straight-line method. Since larger depreciation tax-shields are generated under the accelerated method in the earlier years, the present value of the tax-shields using the accelerated method is more valuable than the present value of the tax-shields using the straight-line method. How much more? $796.

CHANGE IN WORKING CAPITAL

Working capital consists of short-term assets, also referred to as *current assets*, that support the day-to-day operating activity of the business. *Net working capital* is the difference between current assets and current liabilities. Net working capital is what would be left over if the firm had to pay off its current obligations using its current assets.

The adjustment we make for changes in net working capital is attributable to two sources:

1. A change in current asset accounts for transactions or precautionary needs
2. The use of the accrual method of accounting

An investment may increase the firm's level of operations, resulting in an increase in the net working capital needed. If the investment is to produce a new product, the firm may have to invest more in inventory (raw materials, work-in-process, and finished goods). If to increase sales means extending more credit, then the firm's accounts receivable will increase. If the investment requires maintaining a higher cash balance to handle the increased level of transactions, the firm will need more cash. If the investment makes the firm's production facilities more efficient, it may be able to reduce the level of inventory.

Because of an increase in the level of transactions, the firm may want to keep more cash and inventory on hand. As the level of operations increase, the effect of any fluctuations in demand for goods and services may increase, requiring the firm to keep additional cash and inventory "just in case." The firm may also increase working capital as a precaution because, if there is greater variability of cash and inventory, a greater safety cushion will be needed.

If a project enables the firm to be more efficient or lowers costs, it may lower its investment in cash, marketable securities, or inventory, releasing funds for investment elsewhere.

We also use the change in working capital to adjust accounting income (revenues less expenses) to a cash basis because cash flow is ultimately what we are valuing, not accounting numbers. But since we generally have only the accounting numbers to work from, we use this information, making adjustments to arrive at cash.

To see how this works, let's look at the cash flow from sales. Not every dollar of sales is collected in the year of sale: some customers may pay later. This means that the annual sales figure does not represent the cash inflow from sales, because some of these sales are collected in the next period. This also means that at the end of the year there will be some accounts receivable from customers who have not paid yet.

For example, suppose you expect sales in the first year to increase by $20,000 per month and customers typically take 30 days to pay. The change in cash flow from sales in the first year is not $20,000 $\times$ 12 = $240,000 but rather $20,000 $\times$ 11 = $220,000, because one month's worth of sales has not been collected in cash by the end of the year. You adjust for the difference between what is sold and what is collected in cash by keeping track of the change in working capital, which in this case is the increase in account receivable, as shown below:

Change in revenues	$240,000
Less: increase in accounts receivable	20,000
Change in cash inflow from sales	$220,000

On the other side of the balance sheet, if the firm increases its purchases of raw materials and incurs higher production costs, such as labor, the firm may increase its level of short-term liabilities, such as accounts payable and salary and wages payable. Suppose expenses for materials and supplies are forecasted at $10,000 per month for the first year and it takes the firm 30 days to pay. Expenses for the first year are $10,000 $\times$ 12 = $120,000, yet cash outflow for these expenses is only $10,000 $\times$ 11 = $110,000. Accounts payable increases by $10,000, representing one month's of expenses. The increase in net working capital (increase in accounts payable $\Rightarrow$ increases current liabilities $\Rightarrow$ decreases net working capital) reduces the cost of goods sold to give us the cash outflow from expenses:

Cost of goods sold	$120,000
Less: increase in accounts payable	10,000
Change in cash flow for expenses	$110,000

A new project may have one of three effects on working capital: an increase, a decrease, or no change. Furthermore, working capital may change at the beginning of the project or at any point during the life of the project. For example, as a new product is introduced, sales may be terrific in the first few years, requiring an increase in cash, accounts receivable, and inventory to support these increased sales. But all of this requires an increase in working capital, that is, a cash outflow.

But later sales may fall off as competitors enter the market. As sales and production fall off, the need for the increased cash, accounts receivable, and inventory falls off, also. As cash, accounts receivable, and inventory are reduced, there is a cash inflow in the form of the reduction in the funds that become available for other uses within the firm.

A change in net working capital can be thought of as part of the initial investment, the amount necessary to get the project going. Or it can be considered generally as part of operating activity, the day-to-day business of the firm. So do we classify the cash flow associated with net working capital with the asset acquisition and disposition represented in the new project or with the operating cash flows?

If a project requires a change in the firm's net working capital accounts that persists for the duration of the project — say, an increase in inventory levels starting at the time of the investment — we tend to classify the change as part of the acquisition costs at the beginning of the project and as part of disposition proceeds at the end of project. If the change in net working capital is due to the fact that accrual accounting does not coincide with cash flows, we tend to classify the change as part of the operating cash flows.

In many applications, however, we can arbitrarily classify the change in working capital as either investment cash flows or operating cash flows. And the classification doesn't really matter, since it's the bottom line — the change in net cash flows — that matter. How we classify the change in working capital doesn't affect a project's attractiveness. For purposes of illustrating the calculation of cash lows, we will assume that changes in working capital occur only at the beginning and the end of the project's life. Therefore, changes in working capital will be classified along with acquisition and disposition cash flows in the examples in this chapter.

PUTTING IT ALL TOGETHER

Here's what we need to put together to calculate the change in the firm's operating cash flows related to a new investment we are considering:

- Changes in revenues and expenses
- Cash flow from changes in taxes from changes in revenues and expenses
- Cash flow from changes in cash flows from depreciation tax-shields
- Changes in net working capital

There are many ways of compiling the component cash flow changes to arrive at the change in operating cash flow. We will start by first calculating taxable income, making adjustments for changes in taxes, noncash expenses, and net working capital to arrive at operating cash flow.

Suppose you are evaluating a project that is expected to increase sales by $200,000 and expenses by $150,000. The project's assets will have a $10,000 depreciation expense for tax purposes. If the tax rate is 40%, what is the operating cash flow from this project? As you can see in Exhibit 2, the change in operating cash flow is $34,000.

When we can mathematically represent how to calculate the change in operating cash flows for a project, let's use the symbol "Δ" to indicate "change in":

$$
\begin{aligned}
\Delta OCF &= \text{change in operating cash flow} \\
\Delta R &= \text{change in revenues} \\
\Delta E &= \text{change in expenses}
\end{aligned}
$$

$$\Delta D \quad = \quad \text{change in depreciation}$$
$$\tau \quad = \quad \text{tax rate}$$

The change in the operating cash flow is:

$$\underbrace{\Delta OCF}_{\substack{\text{Change in firm's} \\ \text{operating cash} \\ \text{flow}}} = \underbrace{(\Delta R - \Delta E - \Delta D)(1 - \tau)}_{\substack{\text{Change in} \\ \text{after-tax income}}} + \underbrace{\Delta D}_{\substack{\text{Change in} \\ \text{depreciation}}} \quad (1)$$

We can also write this as:

$$\underbrace{\Delta OCF}_{\substack{\text{Change in} \\ \text{firm's operat-} \\ \text{ing} \\ \text{cash flows}}} = \underbrace{(\Delta R - \Delta E)(1 - \tau)}_{\substack{\text{Change in after-tax} \\ \text{income without} \\ \text{considering depreciation}}} + \underbrace{\Delta D\tau}_{\substack{\text{Change in} \\ \text{depreciation} \\ \text{tax-shield}}} \quad (2)$$

Applying equation (1) to the previous example,

$$\begin{aligned}
\Delta OCF &= \quad (\Delta R - \Delta E - \Delta D)(1 - \tau) \quad + \quad \Delta D \\
&= (\$200,000 - 150,000 - 10,000)(1 - 0.40) + \$10,000 \\
&= \$24,000
\end{aligned}$$

Exhibit 2: An Example of the Calculation of the Change in Operating Cash Flow

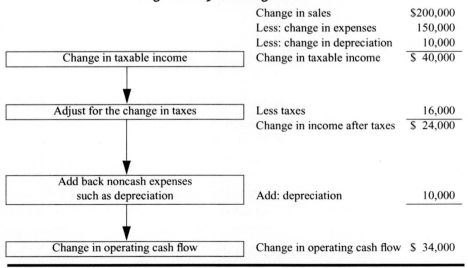

	Change in sales	$200,000
	Less: change in expenses	150,000
	Less: change in depreciation	10,000
Change in taxable income	Change in taxable income	$ 40,000
Adjust for the change in taxes	Less taxes	16,000
	Change in income after taxes	$ 24,000
Add back noncash expenses such as depreciation	Add: depreciation	10,000
Change in operating cash flow	Change in operating cash flow	$ 34,000

Or, using the rearrangement as in equation (2),

$$\Delta OCF \; = \; (\Delta R - \Delta E)\,(1 - \tau) \quad + \quad \Delta D\tau$$
$$= \; (\$200{,}000 - \$150{,}000)\,(1 - 0.40) \; + \; \$10{,}000\,(0.40)$$
$$= \; \$24{,}000$$

Let's look at one more example for the calculation of operating cash flows. Suppose you are evaluating modern equipment that you expect will reduce expenses by $100,000 during the first year. The old machine cost $200,000 and was depreciated using straight-line over 10 years, with five years remaining. The new machine cost $300,000 and will be depreciated using straight-line over ten years. If the firm's tax rate is 30%, what is the expected operating cash flow in the first year?

Let's identify the components:

$\Delta R \; = \; \$0$ ⇐ The new machine does not affect revenues

$\Delta E \; = \; -\$100{,}000$ ⇐ The new machine reduces expenses that will reduce taxes and increase cash flows

$\Delta D \; = \; +\$10{,}000$ ⇐ The new machine increases the depreciation expense from $20,000 to $30,000

$\tau \; = \; 30\%$

The operating cash flow from the first year is therefore:

$$\Delta OCF \; = \; (\Delta R - \Delta E - \Delta D)\,(1 - \tau) \quad + \; \Delta D$$
$$= \; (\$100{,}000 - 10{,}000)\,(1 - 0.30) \; + \; \$10{,}000$$
$$= \; \$63{,}000 \qquad\qquad\qquad\quad + \; \$10{,}000 \; = \; \$73{,}000$$

NET CASH FLOWS

As we have seen, an investment's cash flows consist of two types of cash flows: (1) cash flows related to acquiring and disposing the assets represented in the investment, and (2) cash flows related to operations. To evaluate any investment project, we must consider both cash flows.

The sum of the cash flows from asset acquisition and disposition and from operations is referred to as *net cash flows* (NCF). The net cash flows are therefore the incremental cash flows related to an investment. The net cash flow is calculated for each period of the project's life. In each period, we add the cash flow from asset acquisition and disposition and the cash flow from operations. For a given period,

Net Cash Flow
=Investment cash flow
+ Change in operating cash flow (ΔOCF)

The analysis of the cash flows of investment projects can become quite complex. But by working through any problem systematically, line-by-line, you will be able to sort out the information and focus on those items that determine cash flows.

SIMPLIFICATIONS

To actually analyze a project's cash flows, we need to make several simplifications:

- We assume that cash will flow into or out of the firm at certain points in time, typically at the end of the year, although we realize that cash actually flows into and out of the firm at irregular intervals.
- We assume that the assets are purchased and put to work immediately.
- By combining inflows and outflows in each period, we are assuming that all inflows and outflows in a given period have the same risk.

Since there are so many flows to consider, we focus on flows within a period (say, a year), assuming they all occur at the end of the period. We assume this to reduce the number of things we have to keep track of. Whether or not this assumption matters depends on: (1) the difference between the actual time of cash flow and when we assume it flows at the end of the period (that is, a flow on January 2 is 364 days from December 31, but a flow on December 30 is only one day from December 31), and (2) the opportunity cost of funds. Also, assuming that cash flows occur at specific points in time simplifies the financial mathematics, we use in valuing these cash flows.

Exhibit 3: Capital Budgeting Checklists

Capital Budgeting Checklist Nonreplacement Decision

Investment Cash Flows:
- ❏ Asset cost
- ❏ Shipping and installation costs
- ❏ Asset disposition
- ❏ Tax effect of asset disposition

Cash in Operating Cash Flows:
- ❏ Change in firm's revenues
- ❏ Change in firm's expenses
- ❏ Tax on change in firm's revenues and expenses
- ❏ Depreciation on asset
- ❏ Tax-shield from depreciation
- ❏ Change in working capital to adjust accounting income to cash flows

Capital Budgeting Checklist Replacement Decision

Investment Cash Flows:
- ❏ New asset cost
- ❏ Shipping and installation costs on new asset
- ❏ Old asset disposition
- ❏ Tax effect of old asset disposition
- ❏ New asset disposition
- ❏ Tax effect of new asset disposition
- ❏ Change in working capital (transactions or precautionary needs)

Cash in Operating Cash Flows:
- ❏ Change in firm's revenues
- ❏ Change in firm's expenses
- ❏ Tax on change in firm's revenues and expenses
- ❏ Change in depreciation (new versus old)
- ❏ Tax-shield from change in depreciation
- ❏ Change in working capital to adjust accrual accounting to cash flows

---

Keeping track of the different cash flows of an investment project can be taxing. Developing a checklist of things to consider can help you wade through the analysis of a project's cash flows. Exhibit 3 provides a checklist for the new investment and the replacement investment decisions. When you begin your analysis of an investment decision, take a look at the appropriate checklist to make sure you've covered everything.

Chapter 3

Integrative Examples and Cash Flow Estimation in Practice

I n this chapter, we use two hypothetical examples to illustrate the net cash flow calculations. We conclude the chapter by considering the problems of cash flow estimation in the real world.

INTEGRATIVE EXAMPLE:
THE EXPANSION OF THE WILLIAMS 5 & 10

The Williams 5 & 10 Company is a discount retail chain, selling a variety of goods at low prices. Business has been very good lately, and the Williams 5 & 10 Company is considering opening one more retail outlet in a neighboring town at the end of 1999. Management figures that it would be about five years before a large national chain of discount stores moves into that town to compete with its store. So it is looking at this expansion as a 5-year prospect. After five years, it would most likely retreat from this town.

The Problem

Williams' managers have researched the expansion and determined that the building needed could be built for $400,000 and that it would cost $100,000 to buy the equipment. Under MACRS, the building would be classified as 31.5-year property and depreciated using the straight-line method, with no salvage value. This means that $1/31.5$ of the $400,000 is depreciated each year. Also under MACRS, the equipment would be classified as 5-year property. Management expects to be able to sell the building for $350,000, and the equipment for $50,000, after five years.

The Williams 5 & 10 extends no credit on its sales and pays for all its purchases immediately. The projections for sales and expenses for the new store for the next five years are:

Year	Sales	Expenses
2000	$200,000	$100,000
2001	300,000	100,000
2002	300,000	100,000
2003	300,000	100,000
2004	50,000	20,000

The new store requires $50,000 of additional inventory. Since all sales are in cash, there is no expected increase in accounts receivable. The tax rate is a flat 30%, and there are no tax credits associated with this expansion. Also, capital gains are taxed at the ordinary tax rate.

The Analysis

To determine the relevant cash flows to evaluate this expansion, let's look at this problem bit-by-bit.

> The Williams 5 & 10 Company is a discount retail chain, selling a variety of goods at low prices. Business has been very good lately, and the Williams 5 & 10 Company is considering opening one more retail outlet in a neighboring town at the end of 1999.

This is an expansion of the business into a new market. Since Williams has other similar outlets, this is most likely a low risk type of investment.

> Management figures that it would be about five years before a large national chain of discount stores moves into that town to compete with its store. So it is looking at this expansion as a 5-year prospect. After five years it would most likely retreat from this town.

The economic life of this project is five years. Management expects to expand into this market for only five years, leaving when a competitor enters.

Williams' managers have researched the expansion and determined they the building needed could be built for $400,000 and that it would cost $100,000 to buy the cash registers, shelves, and other equipment necessary to start up this outlet.

The initial outlay for the building and equipment is $500,000. There are no set-up charges, so we can assume that all other initial investment costs are included in these figures.

Under MACRS, the building would be classified as 31.5-year property and depreciated using the straight-line method with no salvage value. This means that $1/31.5$ of the $400,000 is depreciated each year. Also under MACRS, the equipment would be classified as 5-year property.

The depreciation expense for each year is:

Year	Depreciation on the building	Depreciation on the equipment	Total depreciation expenses
1	$12,698	$20,000	$21,698
2	12,698	32,000	44,698
3	12,698	19,200	31,898
4	12,698	11,520	24,218
5	12,698	11,520	24,218
Total	$63,490	$94,240	

The tax bases of the building and equipment at the end of the fifth year are:

Tax basis of building   = $400,000 − 63,490 = $336,510

and

Tax basis of equipment = $100,000 − 94,240 = $5,760

The Williams 5 & 10 Company expects to sell the building for $350,000, and the equipment for $50,000, after five years.

The sale of the building is a cash inflow of $350,000 at the end of the fifth year. The building is expected to be sold for more than its book value, creating a taxable gain of $350,000 − $336,510 = $13,490. The tax on this gain is $4,047.

The sale of the equipment is a cash inflow of $50,000. The gain on the sale of the equipment is $50,000 − $5,760 = $44,240. The tax on this gain is 30% of $44,240, or $13,272.

Williams extends no credit on its sales and pays for all its purchases immediately. The projections for sales and expenses for the new store for the next five years are:

Year	Sales	Expenses
2000	$200,000	$100,000
2001	300,000	100,000
2002	300,000	100,000
2003	300,000	100,000
2004	50,000	20,000

The change in revenues, ΔR, and the change in cash expenses, ΔE, correspond to the sales and costs figures.

The new store would require $50,000 of additional inventory. Since all sales are in cash, there is no expected increase in accounts receivable.

The increase in inventory is an investment of cash when the store is opened: a $50,000 cash outflow. That's the amount Williams has to invest to maintain inventory while the store is in operation. When the store is closed in five years, there is no need to keep this increased level of inventory. If we assume that the inventory at the end of the fifth year can be sold for $50,000, that amount will be a cash inflow at that time. Since this is a change in working capital for the duration of the project, we include this cash flow as part of the asset acquisition (initially) and its disposition (at the end of the fifth year). We will classify the change in inventory as part of the investment cash flows.

The tax rate is a flat 30%, and there are no tax credits associated with this expansion. Also, capital gains are taxed at the ordinary tax rate of 30%.

Once we know the tax rate, we can calculate the cash flows related to acquiring and disposing of assets and the cash flow from operations.

We can calculate the cash flows from operations as:[1]

Year	Change in revenues (ΔR)	Change in expenses (ΔE)	Change in depreciation (ΔD)	Change in income after taxes $(\Delta R - \Delta E - \Delta D)(1 - \tau)$	Change in operating cash flow $(\Delta R - \Delta E - \Delta D)(1 - \tau) + \Delta D$
2001	$200,000	$100,000	$21,698	$54,811	$76,509
2002	300,000	100,000	44,698	108,711	153,409
2003	300,000	100,000	31,898	117,671	149,569
2004	300,000	100,000	24,218	123,047	147,265
2005	50,000	20,000	24,218	4,047	28,265

Or, equivalently, we can calculate the incremental operating cash flows from the new store as:

Year	Change in revenues (ΔR)	Change in expenses (ΔE)	Change in revenues and expenses after taxes $(\Delta R - \Delta E)(1 - \tau)$	Change in depreciation tax-shield ($\Delta D\tau$)	Change in operating cash flow $(\Delta R - \Delta E)(1 - \tau) + \Delta D\tau$
2001	$200,000	$100,000	$70,000	$6,509	$76,509
2002	300,000	100,000	140,000	13,409	153,409
2003	300,000	100,000	140,000	9,569	149,569
2004	300,000	100,000	140,000	7,265	147,265
2005	50,000	20,000	21,000	7,265	28,265

The pieces of this cash flow puzzle are put together in Exhibit 1, which identifies the cash inflows and outflows for each year, with acquisition and disposition cash flows at the top and operating cash flows below. Investing $550,000 initially is expected to result in cash inflows during the following five years. Our next task, which we take up in Section II, is to see whether investing in this project as represented by the cash flows in this time line will increase the owners' wealth.

---

[1] Remember that the changes in working capital have been classified along with acquisition and disposition cash flows.

Exhibit 1: Estimated Incremental Cash Flows from the Williams 5 & 10 Expansion

	Initial	End of year				
		2001	2002	2003	2004	2005
Investment cash flows						
Purchase and sale of building	−$400,000					+$350,000
Tax on sale of building						−4,047
Purchase and sale of equipment	−100,000					+50,000
Tax on sale of equipment						−13,272
Change in working capital	−50,000					+50,000
Investment cash flows	−$550,000					+$432,681
Change in operating cash flows						
Change in revenues, ΔR		+$200,000	+$300,000	+$300,000	+$300,000	+$50,000
Less: Change in expenses, ΔE		−100,000	−100,000	−100,000	−100,000	−20,000
Less: Change in depreciation, ΔD		−32,698	−44,698	−31,898	−24,218	−24,218
Change in taxable income		+$67,302	+$155,302	+$168,102	+$175,782	+$5,782
Less: taxes, $\tau(\Delta R - \Delta E - \Delta D)$		−20,191	−46,591	−50,531	−52,735	−1,735
Change in income after tax, $(1 - \tau)(\Delta R - \Delta E - \Delta D)$		+$47,111	+$108,711	+$117,671	+$123,047	+$4,047
Add: Depreciation, ΔD		+32,698	+44,698	+31,898	+24,218	+24,218
Change in operating cash flows, ΔOCF		+$79,809	+$153,409	+$149,569	+$147,265	+$28,265
Net cash flows	−$550,000	+$79,809	+$153,409	+$149,569	+$147,265	+$460,946

INTEGRATIVE EXAMPLE: THE REPLACEMENT OF FACILITIES AT THE HIRSHLEIFER COMPANY

The management of the Hirshleifer Company is evaluating the replacement of its existing manufacturing equipment with a new equipment. The old equipment cost $200,000 five years ago, currently has a tax basis of $100,000, and has been depreciated on the straight-line basis over a 10-year life, with no salvage value. If Hirshleifer keeps the old equipment, it is expected it to last another five years, at which time the 10-year-old equipment is expected to be sold for $10,000. The old equipment could be sold today for $120,000.

The Problem

The new equipment costs $300,000 and is expected to have a useful life of five years. The new equipment will be depreciated for tax purposes, using MACRS and a 5-year classified life. At the end of its useful life, management expects to sell the new equipment for $100,000. Meanwhile, the new equipment is expected to reduce production costs by $60,000 each year. In addition, since it is more efficient, Hirshleifer can reduce its raw material and work-in-process inventories. Hirshleifer expects to reduce its inventory by $10,000 as soon as the new equipment is placed in service.

The income of Hirshleifer is taxed at a rate of 35%. There are no tax credits available for this equipment. What cash flows would result for each of the five years from this replacement?

The Analysis

This is a replacement project. We need to decide whether to continue with the present equipment or replace it. To do this, we look at the change in cash flows if we replace the equipment, relative to the cash flows of keeping the existing equipment. Instead of analyzing the problem line-by-line, as we did in for the William 5&10, look at the cash flows related to acquiring and disposing assets, and then look at the operating cash flows.

Investment Cash Flows

The new equipment requires an immediate cash outlay of $300,000. It will be depreciated using the specified rates, where 20.00% + 32.00% + 19.20% + 11.52% + 11.52% = 94.24% of its cost is depreciated by the end of the fifth year. That leaves a tax basis of 5.76% of $300,000, or $17,280. The expected sale price of the new equipment at the end of the fifth year is greater than the equipment's book value, so there is a gain on the sale of the equipment of $100,000 − $17,280 = $82,720.

Since the sales price is less than the original cost, this gain is taxed as a recapture of depreciation at ordinary tax rates. The sale of the new equipment in the fifth year creates a gain of $82,720. The cash outflow for taxes on this gain is 0.35 × $82,720 = $28,952.

The $200,000 cost of the old equipment is a sunk cost and is not directly relevant to our analysis. However, we need to consider the tax basis of the old equipment in computing a gain or loss on its sale. We also need to consider the cost of the old equipment to assess whether any gain on its sale would be a capital gain or a recapture of depreciation.

By selling the old equipment for $120,000, the firm will incur a gain of the selling price less the tax basis, or $120,000 − $100,000 = $20,000. This is a recapture of depreciation — taxed at 35% — since the sales price is less than the original cost, or $200,000.

Disposing of the old equipment has two tax-related cash flows: the tax on the sale of the old equipment when the new equipment is purchased, an outflow of 0.35 × $20,000 = $7,000; and the tax we would have had to pay on the sale of the old equipment in the fifth year, an inflow of 0.35 × $10,000 = $3,500.

If the firm replaces the old equipment today, it foregoes the sale of the equipment in five years for $10,000. We need to consider both the foregone cash flow from this sale, as well as any forgone taxes or tax benefits on this sale.

And let's not forget about the change in net working capital. The reduction in inventory is a cash inflow since inventory can be reduced. If we assume it is reduced immediately, there is a $10,000 cash inflow, initially. Assuming that inventory returns to its previous level at the end of the new equipment's life, there will be a $10,000 cash outflow at the end of the fifth year.

Let's summarize the investment cash flows:

Initially:

Purchase of new equipment	−$300,000
Sale of old equipment	+120,000
Tax on sale of old equipment	−7,000
Decrease in inventory	+10,000
Total investment cash flow	−$177,000

Fifth year:

Sale of new equipment	+$100,000
Tax on sale of new equipment	−28,952
Foregone sale of old equipment	−10,000
Foregone tax on sale of old equipment	+3,500
Increase in inventory	−10,000
Total investment cash flow	+$54,548

Operating Cash Flows

If the old equipment is kept, depreciation would continue to be $200,000/10 years = $20,000 per year for each of the next five years. If it is replaced, there would no longer be this depreciation expense.

The new equipment will be depreciated over five years. Comparing the depreciation expense with the old and the new equipment, we determine the change in the taxes from the change in the depreciation tax-shield:

Year	Rate of depreciation on new equipment	Depreciation expense for the new equipment	Depreciation expense of old equipment	Change in depreciation expenses
1	20.00%	$60,000	$20,000	$40,000
2	32.00%	96,000	20,000	76,000
3	19.20%	57,600	20,000	37,600
4	11.52%	34,560	20,000	14,560
5	11.52%	34,560	20,000	14,560
		$282,720	$100,000	

The reduction in costs is a cash inflow — less cash is paid out with the new, than with the old, equipment. But there is additional taxable income — the new machine will reduce expenses by $60,000 each year, so that increases taxable income by $60,000 each year, increasing taxes each year.

The change in operating cash is

Year	Change in revenues (ΔR)	Change in expenses (ΔE)	Change in depreciation (ΔD)	Change in income after taxes $(\Delta R - \Delta E - \Delta D)$ $(1 - \tau)$	Change in operating cash flow $(\Delta R - \Delta E - \Delta D)(1 - \tau)$ $+ \Delta D$
First	$0	−$60,000	$40,000	$13,000	$53,000
Second	0	−60,000	76,000	−10,400	65,600
Third	0	−60,000	37,600	14,560	52,160
Fourth	0	−60,000	14,560	29,536	44,096
Fifth	0	−60,000	14,560	29,536	44,096

Or, equivalently,

Year	Change in revenues (ΔR)	Change in expenses (ΔE)	Change in revenues and expenses after taxes $(\Delta R - \Delta E)(1 - \tau)$	Change in depreciation tax-shield $\Delta D\tau$	Change in operating cash flow $(\Delta R - \Delta E)(1 - \tau)$ $+ \Delta D$
First	$0	−$60,000	$39,000	$14,000	$53,000
Second	0	−60,000	39,000	26,600	65,600
Third	0	−60,000	39,000	13,160	52,160
Fourth	0	−60,000	39,000	5,096	44,096
Fifth	0	−60,000	39,000	5,096	44,096

The project's cash flows are shown in Exhibit 2. Investing $177,000 initially is expected to generate cash inflows shown in the time line in the next five years. Our task, which we will take up in the next chapter, is to evaluate these cash flows to see whether taking on this project will increase the owners' wealth.

CASH FLOW ESTIMATION IN PRACTICE

Now that we have described how firms ideally estimate cash flows, we turn to the question of how managers actually make these important decisions. Surveys of U.S. corporations provide the following important information: [2]

- The person estimating cash flows is an accountant, an analyst, Treasurer, Controller, Vice-President of Finance, or a person reporting directly to the Treasurer or Vice-President of Finance.

[2] Randolph A. Pohlman, Emmanuel S. Santiago, and F. Lynn Markel, "Cash Flow Estimation Practices of Large Firms," *Financial Management* (Summer 1988): 71–79.

Exhibit 2: Estimated Incremental Cash Flows from the Replacement of Facilities at the Hirshleifer Company

		End of year				
	Initial	Year 1	Year 2	Year 3	Year 4	Year 5
Investment cash flows						
Purchase and sale of new equipment	−$300,000					+$100,000
Tax on sale of new equipment						−28,952
Sale of old equipment	+120,000					−10,000
Tax on sale of old equipment	−7,000					+3,500
Change in working capital	+10,000					−10,000
Investment cash flows	−$177,000					+$54,548
Change in operating cash flows						
Change in revenues, ΔR		$0	$0	$0	$0	$0
Less: Change in expenses, ΔE		+60,000	+60,000	+60,000	+60,000	+60,000
Less: Change in depreciation, ΔD		−40,000	−76,000	−37,600	−14,560	−14,560
Change in taxable income		−$20,000	−$16,000	+$22,400	+$45,440	+$45,440
Less: taxes, $\tau(\Delta R - \Delta E - \Delta D)$		+7,000	+5,600	−7,840	−15,904	−15,904
Change in income after tax, $(1 - \tau)(\Delta R - \Delta E - \Delta D)$		−$13,000	−$10,400	+$14,560	+$29,536	+$29,536
Add: Depreciation, ΔD		+40,000	+76,000	+37,600	+14,560	+14,560
Change in operating cash flows, ΔOCF		+$53,000	+$65,600	+$52,160	+$44,096	+$44,096
Net cash flows	−$177,000	+$53,000	+$65,600	+$52,160	+$44,096	+$98,644

- Most firms have standard procedures for estimating cash flows.
- Most firms rely mainly on the subjective judgment of management.
- Most firms consider working capital requirements in their analysis of cash flows.
- Sales and operating-expense forecasts are key ingredients in estimating cash flows.

Estimating cash flows for capital projects is perhaps the most difficult part of the investment screening and selection process. With regard to the process of capital budgeting, most firms use some type of postcompletion auditing, yet few firms have well developed, sophisticated systems for evaluating ongoing projects.[3]

We know that it is necessary to consider cash flows related to acquiring the assets, to disposing of the assets, and to operations. In our analysis, we must not forget to consider working capital and the cash flows related to taxes. But all the while, we are working with estimates — forecasts of the future. Thus, when managers estimate cash flows, they rely on their best guess as to:

- The cost of the assets
- The benefits or costs of disposing the assets at the end of the project
- Sales in each future period
- Expenses in each future period
- Tax rates in each future period
- Working capital needs in each future period

Implicit in cash flow forecasts are judgements pertaining to:

- Competitors' reactions to the investment
- Changes in the tax code
- The costs of materials and labor
- The time it takes to get the project underway

---

[3] Kimberly J. Smith, "Postauditing Capital Investments," *Financial Practice and Education* (Spring/Summer 1994): 129–137.

Looking at how cash flows are estimated, we see that corporations analyze all the key elements — sales, expenses, taxes, and working capital — yet apply judgment in arriving at the estimates of these elements. Thus, cash flow estimation does not lend itself well to the application of mechanical formulas. Though managers can apply formulas that help them put the key elements together, they must always remember that cash flow estimates are determined, in large part, through marketing analyses, engineering studies, and, most importantly, managerial experience.

Case for Section I

THE VILLARD ELECTRIC COMPANY

The financial manager of the Villard Electric Company, Fred Taylor, has presented his estimates of cash flows resulting from the possible investment in a new computer system, the Webnet. Mr. Taylor's estimates of net cash flows immediately and over the following four years are as follows:

Item	Initial	First year	Second year	Third year	Fourth year
Purchase of computer system	−$200,000				
Sale of computer system					$40,000
Tax on sale of computer system					12,442
Acquisition and disposition cash flows	−$200,000	$0	$0	$0	$52,442
Change in expenses		$50,000	$50,000	$50,000	$50,000
Change in depreciation		40,000	64,000	38,400	23,040
Change in taxable income		$10,000	−$14,000	$11,600	$26,960
Less: change in tax		3,600	−5,040	4,176	9,706
Change in income after tax		$6,400	−$8,960	$7,424	$17,254
Change in depreciation		40,000	64,000	38,400	23,040
Change in operating cash flows		$46,400	$55,040	$45,824	$40,294
Change in net cash flows	−$200,000	$46,400	$55,040	$45,824	$92,736

Mr. Taylor has based his estimates on the following assumptions:

- The cost of the system (including installation) is $200,000.
- The system will be depreciated as a 5-year asset under the MACRS, but it will be sold at the end of the fourth year for $50,000.
- Villard's expenses will decline by $50,000 in each of the four years.
- The company's tax rate will be 36%.
- Working capital will not be affected.

When he made his presentation to Villard's board of directors, Mr. Taylor was asked to perform additional analyses to consider the following uncertainties:

- The cost of the system may be as much as 20% higher or as low as 20% lower.
- The change in expenses may be 30% higher or 20% lower than anticipated.
- The tax rate may be lowered to 30%.

Requirements

a. Reestimate the project's cash flows to consider each of the possible variations in the assumptions, altering only one assumption each time. Using a spreadsheet program will help with the calculations.

b. Discuss the impact that each of the changes in assumptions has on the project's cash flows.

Questions for Section I

1. How does an investment in a then-new product five years ago affect the value of the firm today?

2. Why might the economic life of an asset be shorter than its actual, physical, expected life?

3. While the objective of short-term and long-term investments are the same, the approaches we use to analyze these two types of investments are different. Why would the approaches to analyzing our investment in cash — the amount of cash we have on hand — be different than our investment in a new product?

4. Suppose a toy manufacturer is faced with the following collection of investment projects:
   (a) Opening a retail outlet
   (b) Introducing a new line of dolls
   (c) Introducing a new action figure in an existing line of action figures
   (d) Adding another packaging line to the production process
   (e) Adding pollution control equipment to avoid environmental fines
   (f) Computerizing the doll-molding equipment
   (g) Introducing a child's version of an existing adult board game

   Classify each project into one of the four categories: expansion, replacement, new product or market, or mandated.

5. A shoe manufacturer is considering introducing a new line of boots. When evaluating the incremental revenues from this new line, what should be considered?

6. If you sell an asset for more than its tax basis, but less than its original cost, we refer to this gain as a recapture of depreciation and it is taxed at ordinary income tax rates. Why?

7. How does a capital loss on the disposition of an asset generate a cash inflow?

8. If a project's projected revenues and expenses are on a cash basis, is there any need to adjust for a change in working capital? Explain.

9. If a firm replaces its production line with equipment with lower depreciation expenses, will the tax cash flow from depreciation be an inflow or an outflow? Explain.

10. Classify each of the following changes as increasing or decreasing the operating cash flow:
    (a) An increase in Raw Materials Inventory
    (b) An increase in Salaries and Wages payable
    (c) An increase in Accounts Receivable
    (d) An increase in Raw Materials Inventory
    (e) A decrease in Accounts Receivable
    (f) A decrease in Accounts Payable
    (g) A decrease in Finished Goods Inventory
    (h) A decrease in Accounts receivable

11. Depreciation does not involve a cash flow, yet we consider cash flows from the depreciation tax-shield. What is the depreciation tax-shield, and how does it produce a cash flow?

12. Suppose a firm buys an asset, depreciates it over its 10-year MACRS life, and then sells it for $100,000 15 years from the time it had bought it. Without performing any calculations, describe the tax consequences related to the asset's purchase, depreciation, and sale.

Problems for Section I

1. Suppose you buy an asset for $1,000,000. If it costs $100,000 for shipping and installation, how much is your investment outlay?

2. Suppose you buy an asset for $100,000 that is depreciated for tax purposes over 20 years using straight-line depreciation. Break down the tax effects upon sale of this asset after five years if the sales price is: (a) $125,000 (b) $100,000 (c) $75,000 (d) $50,000

3. The Schwab Steel Company is considering two different wire soldering machines. Machine 1 has an initial cost of $100,000, costs $20,000 to set up and is expected to be sold for $20,000 after 10 years. Machine 2 has an initial cost of $80,000, costs $30,000 to set up and is expected to be sold for $10,000 after 10 years. Both machines would be depreciated over 10 years using straight-line depreciation. Schwab has a tax rate of 35%.
   (a) What are the cash flows related to the acquisition of each machine?
   (b) What are the cash flows related to the disposition of each machine?

4. The Tinbergen Company is considering a new polishing machine. The existing polishing machine cost $100,000 five years ago and is being depreciated using straight-line over a 10-year life. Tinbergen's management estimates that they can sell the old machine for $60,000. The new machine costs $150,000 and would be depreciated over five years using MACRS. At the end of the fifth year, Tinbergen's management expects to be able to sell the new polishing machine for $75,000. The marginal tax rate is 40%.
   (a) What are the cash flows related to the acquisition of the new machine?
   (b) What are the cash flows related to the disposition of the old machine?
   (c) What are the cash flows related to the disposition of the new machine?

5. Mama's Goulash Company is considering purchasing a dishwasher. The dishwasher costs $50,000 and would be depreciated over three years using MACRS. After three years, Mama's plans to sell the dishwasher for $10,000. The marginal tax rate is 40%.
   (a) What are the cash flows related to the acquisition of the dishwasher?
   (b) What are the cash flows related to the disposition of the dishwasher?

6. If an investment is expected to increase revenues by $100,000 per year for five years, with no effect on expenses or working capital, what is the operating cash flow per year if depreciation is $20,000 each year and the tax rate is: (a) 20%? (b) 30%? (c) 40%? (d) 50%?

7. The Gomez Mustache Wax Company is evaluating the purchase of a new wax-molding machine. The machine costs $100,000 and has a useful life of five years. How do the cash flows differ when straight-line is used instead of MACRS depreciation for tax purposes, assuming a tax rate of 40% and no salvage value?

8. Calculate the change in operating cash flow for each year using the following information:

   • The machine costs $1,000,000 and is depreciated using straight-line over five years.
   • The machine will increase sales by $150,000 per year for five years.
   • The tax rate is 40%.
   • Working capital needs increase by $10,000 when the machine is placed in service and are reduced at the end of the life of the machine.
   • There is no salvage value at the end of the five years.

9. Calculate the change in operating cash flow for each year using the following information:

   • The equipment costs $200,000 and is depreciated using MACRS over five years.

- The equipment will reduce operating expenses by $25,000 per year for five years.
- The tax rate is 30%.
- Working capital needs increase by $10,000 when the machine is placed in service and are reduced at the end of the life of the machine.
- There is no salvage value at the end of five years.

10. Calculate the change in operating cash flow for a firm for each year using the following information:

- The asset costs $1,000,000 and is depreciated using MACRS for a 3-year asset.
- The machine will reduce operating expenses by $120,000 per year for three years.
- The tax rate is 45%.
- Working capital needs decrease by $10,000 when the machine is placed in service and are increased at the end of the life of the machine.
- The asset can be sold for $400,000 at the end of three years.

11. The Smith Company is a beauty products company that is considering a new hair growth product. This new product would encourage hair growth for persons with thinning hair. The new product is expected to generate sales of $500,000 per year and would cost $300,000 to produce each year. It is expected that the patent on the new product would prevent competition from entering the market for at least seven years.

Smith Company spent $1,000,000 developing the new product over the past four years. The equipment to produce the new product would cost $1,500,000 and would be depreciated for tax purposes as a 5-year MACRS asset. Smith's management estimates that the equipment could be sold after seven years for $400,000. The marginal tax rate for Smith Company is 40%.

(a) What are the initial cash flows related to the new product?

(b) What are the cash flows related to the disposition of the equipment after seven years?

(c) What are the operating cash flows for each year?

(d) What are the net cash flows for each year?

12. The Nobel Dynamite Company is considering a new packing machine. The existing packing machine cost $500,000 five years ago and is being depreciated using straight-line over a 10-year life. Nobel's management estimates that the old machine can be sold for $100,000. The new machine costs $600,000 and would be depreciated over five years using straight-line. There is no salvage value for the new machine. The new machine is more efficient and would reduce packing expenses (damaged goods) by $120,000 per year for the next five years. The marginal tax rate is 30%.

(a) What are the cash flows related to the acquisition of the new machine?

(b) What are the cash flows related to the disposition of the old machine?

(c) What are the cash flows related to the disposition of the new machine?

(d) What are the operating cash flows for each year?

(e) What are the net cash flows for each year?

13. The J. J. Hill Company is considering new digging equipment machine. The existing digging equipment cost $1,000,000 five years ago and is being depreciated using MACRS, when classified as a 5-year asset. Hill's management estimates the old equipment can be sold for $200,000. The new equipment costs $1,200,000 and would be depreciated over five years using MACRS. At the end of the fifth year, Hill's management intends to sell the new equipment for $400,000. The new equipment is more efficient and would reduce expenses by $200,000 per year for the next five years. The marginal tax rate is 35%.

(a) What are the cash flows related to the acquisition of the new equipment?

(b) What are the cash flows related to the disposition of the old equipment?

(c) What are the cash flows related to the disposition of the new equipment?

(d) What are the operating cash flows for each year?

(e) What are the net cash flows for each year?

14. The NeaterMaid Cleaning Service Company is considering replacing its existing cleaning equipment. The existing equipment cost $100,000 five years ago and was depreciated using MACRS as a 3-year asset. The management of NeaterMaid estimates the old equipment can be sold for $10,000. The new equipment costs $120,000 and would be depreciated using MACRS for a 3-year asset. At the end of five years, NeaterMaid's management expects to sell the new equipment for $200,000. The new equipment is more efficient and would reduce expenses by $20,000 per year for the next five years. The marginal tax rate is 30%.

(a) What are the cash flows related to the acquisition of the new equipment?

(b) What are the cash flows related to the disposition of the old equipment?

(c) What are the cash flows related to the disposition of the new equipment?

(d) What are the operating cash flows for each year?

(e) What are the net cash flows for each year?

15. Consider a project that is expected to reduce expenses each year for the next five years by $1 million. After considering taxes, what is the contribution to operating cash flows solely from the change in expenses from this project if the tax rate is 30%?

16. The Jonhaux Trading Company is considering a project that will change its working capital accounts in the following manner:

Account	Direction of change	Amount of change
Cash	Increase	$10,000
Accounts receivable	Increase	$30,000
Inventory	Reduce	$20,000
Accounts payable	Increase	$5,000

Calculate the change in Jonhaux's cash flows resulting from the change in the working capital accounts.

17. Suppose that you are evaluating an asset that costs $400,000 and that is depreciated for tax purposes using MACRS rates for a 5-year asset. Assume a marginal tax rate of 30%.
    (a) What is the amount of the depreciation expense in the second year?
    (b) What is the amount of the depreciation tax-shield in the second year?
    (c) If you plan to dispose of the asset at the end of the third year, what is the asset's tax basis at the time of sale?
    (d) If you can sell the asset for $50,000 at the end of the fifth year, do you have a gain or a loss? What are the tax consequences of this sale? What are the cash flow consequences?
    (e) If you can sell the asset for $100,000 at the end of the fifth year, do you have a gain or a loss? What are the tax consequences of this sale? What are the cash flow consequences?

18. The president of Cook Airlines has asked you to evaluate the proposed acquisition of a new jet. The jet's price is $40 million, and it is classified in the 10-year MACRS class. The purchase of the jet would require an increase in net working capital of $200,000. The jet would increase the firm's before-tax revenues by $20 million per year but would also increase operating costs by $5 million per year. The jet is expected to be used for three years and then sold for $25 million. The firm's marginal tax rate is 40%.
    (a) What is the amount of the investment outlay required at the beginning of the project?
    (b) What is the amount of the operating cash flow each year?
    (c) What is the amount of the nonoperating cash flow in the third year?
    (d) What is the amount of the net cash flow for each year?

Section II

Capital Budgeting Evaluation Techniques

The value of a firm today is the present value of all its future cash flows. These future cash flows come from assets that are already in place and from future investment opportunities. These future cash flows are discounted at a rate that represents investors' assessments of the uncertainty that they will flow in the amounts and when expected:

$$\text{Value of firm} = \text{Present value of all future cash flows}$$
$$= \text{Present value of cash flows from all assets in place}$$
$$+ \text{Present value of cash flows from future investment opportunities}$$

The objective of the financial manager is to maximize the value of the firm and, therefore, owners' wealth. As we saw in the previous chapter, the financial manager makes decisions regarding long-lived assets in the process referred to as *capital budgeting*. The capital budgeting decisions for a project requires analysis of:

- Its future cash flows
- The degree of uncertainty associated with these future cash flows
- The value of these future cash flows considering their uncertainty

We looked at how to estimate cash flows in Section I in which we were concerned with a project's incremental cash flows. These comprise changes in operating cash flows (change in revenues, expenses, and taxes) and changes in investment cash flows (the firm's incremental cash flows from the acquisition and disposition of the project's assets).

In Section II, we introduce the second required element of capital budgeting: *risk*. In the study of valuation principles, we saw that the more uncertain a future cash flow, the less it is worth today. The degree of uncertainty, or risk, is reflected in a project's cost of capital. The *cost of capital* is what the firm must pay for the funds needed to finance an investment. The cost of capital may be an explicit cost (for example, the interest paid on debt) or an implicit cost (for example, the expected price appreciation of shares of the firm's common stock).

In Chapter 4, we focus on the third element of capital budgeting: valuing the future cash flows. Given estimates of incremental cash flows for a project and given a cost of capital that reflects the project's risk, we look at alternative techniques that are used to select projects.

For now, we will incorporate risk into our calculations in either of two ways: (1) we can discount future cash flows using a higher discount rate, the greater the cash flow's risk, or (2) we can require a higher annual return on a project, the greater the risk of its cash flows. We will look at specific ways of estimating risk and incorporating risk in the discount rate in Section III.

The following exhibit shows four pairs of projects for evaluation in the chapters in this section.

Investments A and B	*Investments E and F*
Each requires an investment of $1,000,000 at the end of the year 2000 and have a cost of capital of 10% per year.	Each requires $1,000,000 at the end of the year 2000 and have a cost of capital of 5% per year.

Year	End-of-Year Cash Flow	
	Investment A	Investment B
2001	$400,000	$100,000
2002	400,000	100,000
2003	400,000	100,000
2004	400,000	1,000,000
2005	400,000	1,000,000

Year	End-of-Year Cash Flows	
	Investment E	Investment F
2001	$300,000	$0
2002	300,000	0
2003	300,000	0
2004	300,000	1,200,000
2005	300,000	200,000

Investments C and D

Each requires $1,000,000 at the end of the year 2000 and have a cost of capital of 10% per year.

	End-of-Year Cash Flows	
Year	Investment C	Investment D .
2001	$300,000	$300,000
2002	300,000	300,000
2003	300,000	300,000
2004	300,000	300,000
2005	300,000	10,000,000

Investments G and H

Each requires $1,000,000 at the end of the year 2000. Investment G has a cost of capital of 5% per year; investment H's cost of capital is 10% per year.

	End-of-Year Cash Flows	
Year	Investment G	Investment H
2001	$250,000	$250,000
2002	250,000	250,000
2003	250,000	250,000
2004	250,000	250,000
2005	250,000	250,000

Look at the incremental cash flows for investments A and B shown in the exhibit. Can you tell by looking at the cash flows for investment A whether or not it enhances wealth? Or, can you tell by just looking at investments A and B which one is better? Perhaps with some projects you may think you can pick out which one is better simply by gut feeling or eyeballing the cash flows. But why do it that way when there are precise methods to evaluate investments by their cash flows?

To evaluate investment projects and select the one that maximizes wealth, we must determine the cash flows from each investment and then assess the uncertainty of all the cash flows. In this section, we look at six techniques that are commonly used to evaluate investments in long-term assets:

1. Payback period
2. Discounted payback period
3. Net present value
4. Profitability index
5. Internal rate of return
6. Modified internal rate of return

We are interested in how well each technique discriminates among the different projects, steering us toward the projects that maximize owners' wealth.

An evaluation technique should consider all the following elements of a capital project:

- All the future incremental cash flows from the project
- The time value of money
- The uncertainty associated with future cash flows

Projects selected using a technique that satisfies all three criteria will, under most general conditions, maximize owners' wealth. Such a technique should include objective rules to determine which project or projects to select.

In addition to judging whether each technique satisfies these criteria, we will also look at which ones can be used in special situations, such as when a dollar limit is placed on the capital budget. We will demonstrate each technique and determine in what way, and how well, it evaluates each of the projects described in the Exhibit above.

Chapter 4

Payback and Discounted Payback Period Techniques

I n this chapter we will discuss the payback period technique and a variant of this technique, the discounted payback period.

PAYBACK PERIOD

The *payback period* for a project is the length of time it takes to get your money back. It is the period from the initial cash outflow to the time when the project's cash inflows add up to the initial cash outflow. The payback period is also referred to as the *payoff period* or the *capital recovery period*. If you invest $10,000 today and are promised $5,000 one year from today and $5,000 two years from today, the payback period is two years — it takes two years to get your $10,000 investment back.

Suppose you are considering investments A and B in Exhibit 1, each requiring an investment of $1,000,000 today (we're considering today to be the last day of the year 2000) and promising cash flows at the end of each of the following five years. How long does it take to get your $1,000,000 investment back? The payback period for investment A is three years:

End of Year	Expected Cash Flow	Accumulated Cash Flow	
2001	$400,000	$400,000	
2002	400,000	800,000	
2003	400,000	1,200,000	⇦ $1,000,000 investment is paid back
2004	400,000	1,600,000	
2005	400,000	2,000,000	

By the end of 2002, the full $1 million is not paid back, but by 2003, the accumulated cash flow exceeds $1 million. Therefore, the payback period for investment A is three years. Using a similar approach of comparing the investment outlay with the accumulated cash flow, the payback period for investment B is four years — it is not until the end of 2004 that the $1,000,000 original investment (and more) is paid back.

We have assumed that the cash flows are received at the end of the year. So we always arrive at a payback period in terms of a whole number of years. If we assume that the cash flows are received, say, uniformly, such as monthly or weekly, throughout the year, we arrive at a payback period in terms of years and *fractions* of years. For example, assuming we receive cash flows uniformly throughout the year, the payback period for investment A is 2 years and 6 months, and the payback period for investment B is 3.7 years, or 3 years and 8.5 months. Our assumption of end-of-period cash flows may be unrealistic, but it is convenient to demonstrate how to use the various evaluation techniques. We will continue to use this end-of-period assumption throughout this chapter.

Payback Period Decision Rule

Is investment A or B more attractive? A shorter payback period is better than a longer payback period. Yet there is no clear-cut rule for how short is better. Investment A provides a quicker payback than B. But that doesn't mean it provides the better value for the firm. All we know is that A "pays for itself" quicker than B. We do not know in this particular case whether quicker is better.

In addition to having no well-defined decision criteria, payback period analysis favors investments with "front-loaded" cash flows: an investment looks better in terms of the payback period the sooner its cash flows are received, no matter what its later cash flows look like!

Payback period analysis is a type of "break-even" measure. It tends to provide a measure of the economic life of the investment in terms of its payback period. The more likely the life exceeds the payback period, the more attractive the investment. The economic life beyond the payback period is referred to as the *postpayback duration*. If postpayback duration is zero, the investment is worthless, *no matter how short the payback*. This is because the sum of the future cash flows is no greater than the initial investment outlay.

And since these future cash flows are really worth less today than in the future, a zero postpayback duration means that the present value of the future cash flows is *less* than the project's initial investment.

Payback should only be used as a coarse initial screen of investment projects. But it can be a useful indicator of some things. Since a dollar of cash flow in the early years is worth more than a dollar of cash flow in later years, the payback period method provides a simple, yet crude measure of the value of the investment.

The payback period also offers some indication of risk. In industries where equipment becomes obsolete rapidly or where there are very competitive conditions, investments with earlier payback are more valuable. That's because cash flows farther into the future are more uncertain and therefore have lower present value. In the personal computer industry, for example, the fierce competition and rapidly changing technology requires investment in projects that have a payback of less than one year, since there is no expectation of project benefits beyond one year.

Further, the payback period gives us a rough measure of the liquidity of the investment (how soon we get cash flows from our investment). However, because the payback method doesn't tell us the particular payback period that maximizes wealth, we cannot use it as the primary screening device for investment in long-lived assets.

Payback Period as an Evaluation Technique
Let's look at the payback period technique in terms of the three criteria listed earlier.

Criterion 1: Does Payback Consider All Cash Flows?
Look at investments C and D in Exhibit 1 and let's assume that their cash flows have similar risk, require an initial outlay of $1,000,000, and have cash flows at the end of each year. Both investments have a payback period of four years. If we used only the payback period to evaluate them, it's likely we would conclude that both investments are identical. Yet, investment D is more valuable because of the cash flow of $10,000,000 in 2005. The payback method *ignores* the $10,000,000! We know C and D cannot be equal. Certainly investment D's $10 million in the year 2005 is more valuable in 2000 than investment C's $300,000.

Criterion 2: Does Payback Consider the Timing of Cash Flows?

Look at investments E and F. They have similar risk, require an investment of $1,000,000, and have the expected end-of-year cash flows described in Exhibit 1. The payback period of both investments is four years. But the cash flows of investment F are received later in the 4-year period than those of investment E. We know that there is a time-value to money — receiving money sooner is better than later — that is not considered in a payback evaluation. The payback period method ignores the timing of cash flows.

Criterion 3: Does Payback Consider the Riskiness of Cash Flows?

Look at investments G and H. Each requires an investment of $1,000,000 and has identical cash inflows. If we assume that the cash flows of investment G are less risky than the cash flows of investment H, can the payback period help us to decide which is preferred?

The payback period of both investments is four years. The payback period is *identical* for these two investments, even though the cash flows of investment H are riskier and therefore less valuable today than those of investment G. But we know that the more uncertain the future cash flow, the less valuable it is today. The payback period ignores the risk associated with the cash flows.

Is Payback Consistent with Owners' Wealth Maximization?

There is no connection between an investment's payback period and its profitability. The payback period evaluation ignores the time value of money, the uncertainty of future cash flows, and the contribution of a project to the value of the firm. Therefore, the payback period method is not going to indicate projects that maximize owners' wealth.

DISCOUNTED PAYBACK PERIOD

The *discounted payback period* is the time needed to pay back the original investment in terms of *discounted* future cash flows. Each cash flow is discounted back to the beginning of the investment at a rate that reflects both the time value of money and the uncertainty of the future cash flows. This rate is the cost of capital, that is, the return required by the suppliers of capital (creditors and owners) to compensate them for the time value of money and the risk associated with the investment. The more uncertain the future cash flows, the greater the cost of capital.

From the perspective of the investor, the cost of capital is the *required rate of return* (RRR), the return that suppliers of capital demand on their investment (adjusted for tax deductibility of interest). Since the cost of capital and the RRR are basically the same concept, but from different perspectives, we sometimes use the terms interchangeably in our study of capital budgeting.

Returning to investments A and B, suppose that each has a cost of capital of 10%. The first step in determining the discounted payback period is to discount each year's cash flow to the beginning of the investment (the end of the year 2000) at the cost of capital:

	Investment A		Investment B	
Year	End-of-year cash flow	Value at the end of 2000	End-of-year cash flow	Value at the end of 2000
2001	$400,000	$363,636	$100,000	$90,909
2002	400,000	330,579	100,000	82,644
2003	400,000	300,526	100,000	75,131
2004	400,000	273,205	1,000,000	683,013
2005	400,000	248,369	1,000,000	620,921

How long does it take for each investment's discounted cash flows to pay back its $1,000,000 investment? The discounted payback period for A is four years:

End of Year	Value at the end of 2000	Accumulated discounted cash flows	
2001	$363,640	$363,640	
2002	330,580	694,220	
2003	300,530	994,750	
2004	273,205	1,267,955	⇦ $1,000,000 investment paid back
2005	248,369	1,516,324	

The discounted payback period for B is five years:

End of Year	Investment B	
	Value at the end of 2000	Accumulated discounted cash flows
2001	$90,910	$90,910
2002	86,240	177,150
2003	75,130	252,280
2004	683,010	935,290
2005	620,921	1,556,211	⇐ $1,000,000 investment paid back

This example shows that it takes one more year to pay back each investment with discounted cash flows than with nondiscounted cash flows.

Discounted Payback Decision Rule

It appears that the shorter the payback period, the better, whether using discounted or nondiscounted cash flows. But how short is better? We don't know. All we know is that an investment "breaks even" in terms of discounted cash flows at the discounted payback period — the point in time when the accumulated discounted cash flows equal the amount of the investment. Using the length of the payback as a basis for selecting investments, A is preferred to B. But we've ignored some valuable cash flows for both investments.

Discounted Payback as an Evaluation Technique

Here is how discounted payback measures up against the three criteria.

Criterion 1: Does Discounted Payback Consider All Cash Flows?

Look again at investments C and D. The main difference between them is that D has a very large cash flow in 2005, relative to C. Discounting each cash flow at the 10% cost of capital,

Year	Investment C		Investment D	
	End-of-year cash flow	Value at the end of 2000	End-of-year cash flow	Value at the end of 2000
2001	$300,000	$272,727	$300,000	$272,727
2002	300,000	247,934	300,000	247,934
2003	300,000	225,394	300,000	225,394
2004	300,000	204,904	300,000	204,904
2005	300,000	186,276	10,000,000	6,209,213

The discounted payback period for C is four years:

End of Year	Investment C	
	Value at the end of 2000	Accumulated discounted cash flows
2001	$272,727	$272,727
2002	247,934	520,661
2003	225,394	746,055
2004	204,904	950,959
2005	186,276	1,137,235

⇦ $1,000,000 investment paid back

The discounted payback period for D is also four years, with each year-end cash flow from 2001 through 2004 contributing the same as those of investment C. However, D's cash flow in 2005 contributes over $6 million more in terms of the present value of the project's cash flows:

End of Year	Investment D	
	Value at the end of 2000	Accumulated discounted cash flows
2001	$272,727	$272,727
2002	247,934	520,661
2003	225,394	746,055
2004	204,904	950,959
2005	6,209,213	7,160,172

⇦ $1,000,000 investment paid back

The discounted payback period method *ignores* the remaining discounted cash flows: $950,959 + $186,276 − $1,000,000 = $137,236 from investment C in year 2005 and $950,959 + $6,209,213 − $1,000,000 = $6,160,172 from investment D in year 2005.

Criterion 2: Does Discounted Payback Consider the Timing of Cash Flows?
Look at investments E and F. Using a cost of capital of 5% for both E and F, the discounted cash flows for each period are:

Year	Investment E		Investment F	
	End-of-year cash flow	Value at the end of 2000	End-of-year cash flow	Value at the end of 2000
2001	$300,000	$285,714	$0	$0
2002	300,000	272,109	0	0
2003	300,000	259,151	0	0
2004	300,000	246,811	1,200,000	987,243
2005	300,000	235,058	300,000	235,058

The discounted payback period for E is four years:

End of Year	Investment E Value at the end of 2000	Accumulated discounted cash flows	
2001	$285,714	$285,714	
2002	272,109	557,823	
2003	259,151	816,974	
2004	246,811	1,063,785	⇦ $1,000,000 investment paid back
2005	235,058	1,298,843	

The discounted payback period for F is five years:

End of Year	Investment F Value at the end of 2000	Accumulated discounted cash flows	
2001	$0	$0	
2002	0	0	
2003	0	0	
2004	$987,243	$987,243	
2005	235,058	1,222,301	⇦ $1,000,000 investment paid back

The discounted payback period is able to distinguish investments with different timing of cash flows. E's cash flows are expected sooner than those of F. E's discounted payback period is shorter than F's — four years versus five years.

Criterion 3: Does Discounted Payback Consider the Riskiness of Cash Flows?

Look at investments G and H. Suppose the cost of capital for G is 5% and the cost of capital for H is 10%. We are assuming that H's cash flows are more uncertain than G's. The discounted cash flows for the two investments, using the appropriate discount rate, are:

Year	Investment G End-of-year cash flow	Value at the end of 2000	Investment H End-of-year cash flow	Value at the end of 2000
2001	$250,000	$238,095	$250,000	$227,273
2002	250,000	226,757	250,000	206,612
2003	250,000	215,959	250,000	187,829
2004	250,000	205,676	250,000	170,753
2005	250,000	195,882	250,000	155,230

The discounted payback period for G is five years:

End of Year	Investment G	
	Value at the end of 2000	Accumulated discounted cash flows
2001	$238,095	$238,095
2002	226,757	464,852
2003	215,959	680,811
2004	205,676	886,487
2005	195,882	1,082,369

⇐ $1,000,000 investment paid back

According to the discounted payback period method, H does not pay back its original $1,000,000 investment — not in terms of discounted cash flows:

End of Year	Investment H	
	Value at the end of 2000	Accumulated discounted cash flows
2001	$227,273	$227,273
2002	206,612	433,885
2003	187,829	621,714
2004	170,753	792,467
2005	155,230	947,697

⇐ Less than $1,000,000 paid back

Since risk is reflected through the discount rate, risk is explicitly incorporated into the discounted payback period analysis. The discounted payback period method is able to distinguish between investment G and the riskier investment H.

Is Discounted Payback Consistent with Owners' Wealth Maximization?

Discounted payback cannot provide us any information about how profitable an investment is — because it ignores everything after the "break-even" point! The discounted payback period can be used as an initial screening device — eliminating any projects that don't pay back over the expected term of the investment. But since it ignores some of the cash flows that contribute to the present value of investment (those above and beyond what is necessary for the investment's payback), the discounted payback period technique is not consistent with owners' wealth maximization.

Chapter 5

Net Present Value Technique

$\mathbf{I}$f offered an investment that costs \$5,000 today and promises to pay you \$7,000 two years from today, and if your opportunity cost for projects of similar risk is 10%, would you make this investment? You need to compare your \$5,000 investment with the \$7,000 cash flow you expect in two years. Since you feel that a discount rate of 10% reflects the degree of uncertainty associated with the \$7,000 expected in two years, today it is worth:

$$\text{Present value of \$7,000 to be received in two years} = \frac{\$7,000}{(1+0.10)^2}$$
$$= \$5,785.12$$

By investing \$5,000 today, you are getting in return a promise of a cash flow in the future that is worth \$5,785.12 today. You increase your wealth by \$785.12 when you make this investment.

NET PRESENT VALUE CALCULATION

Another way of stating this is that the present value of the \$7,000 cash inflow is \$5,785.12, which is more than the \$5,000, today's cash outflow to make the investment. When we subtract today's cash outflow to make an investment from the present value of the cash inflow from the investment, the difference is the increase or decrease in our wealth referred to as the net present value.

The *net present value* (NPV) is the present value of *all* expected cash flows.

Net Present Value = Present value of all expected cash flows

Or, in terms of the incremental operating and investment cash flows,

71

Net Present Value
= Present value of the change in operating cash flows
+ Present value of the investment cash flows

"Net" is the difference between the change in the operating cash flows and the investment cash flows causing the change in the firm's operating cash flows. Often the change in operating cash flows are inflows and the investment cash flows are outflows. Therefore we tend to refer to the net present value as the difference between the present value of the cash inflows and the present value of the cash outflows.

We can represent the net present value using summation notation, where t indicates any particular period, CF_t represents the cash flow at the end of period t, i represents the cost of capital, and T the number of periods making up the economic life of the investment:

$$\text{NPV} = \sum_{t=0}^{N} \frac{CF_t}{(1+i)^t} \tag{1}$$

Cash inflows are positive values of CF_t, and cash outflows are negative values of CF_t. For any given period t, we collect all the cash flows (positive and negative) and net them together. To make things a bit easier to track, let's just refer to cash flows as inflows or outflows and not specifically identify them as operating or investment cash flows.

Let's take another look at investments A and B. Using a 10% cost of capital, the present values of inflows are:

| | Investment A | | Investment B | |
| | End-of-year | Value at the | End-of-year | Value at the |
Year	cash flow	end of 2000	cash flow	end of 2000
2001	$400,000	$363,636	$100,000	$90,909
2002	400,000	330,579	100,000	82,645
2003	400,000	300,526	100,000	75,131
2004	400,000	273,206	1,000,000	683,013
2005	400,000	248,369	1,000,000	620,921
Present value of the cash inflows		$1,516,315		$1,552,620

The present value of the cash outflows is the outlay of $1,000,000. The net present value of A is $516,315:

NPV of A = $1,516,315 − $1,000,000 = $516,315

and the net present value of B is $552,620:

$$NPV \text{ of } B = \$1,552,620 - \$1,000,000 = \$552,620$$

These NPVs tell us if we invest in A, we expect to increase the value of the firm by $516,315. If we invest in B, we expect to increase the value of the firm by $552,620.

NET PRESENT VALUE DECISION RULE

A positive net present value means that the investment increases the value of the firm — the return is more that sufficient to compensate for the required return of the investment. A negative net present value means that the investment decreases the value of the firm — the return is less than the cost of capital. A zero net present value means that the return just equals the return required by owners to compensate them for the degree of uncertainty of the investment's future cash flows and the time value of money. Therefore,

if...	this means that...	and you...
NPV > 0	the investment is expected to increase shareholder wealth	should accept the project.
NPV < 0	the investment is expected to decrease shareholder wealth	should reject the project.
NPV = 0	the investment is expected not to change shareholder wealth	are indifferent between accepting or rejecting the project.

Investment A increases the value of the firm by $516,315 and B increases it by $552,620. If these are independent investments, both should be taken on because both increase the value of the firm. If A and B are *mutually exclusive*, such that the only choice is either A or B, then B is preferred since it has the greater NPV.

NET PRESENT VALUE AS AN EVALUATION TECHNIQUE

Now let's compare the net present value technique in terms of the three criteria.

Criterion 1: Does Net Present Value Consider All Cash Flows?
Look at investments C and D, which are similar except for the cash
flows in 2005. The net present value of each investment, using a
10% cost of capital, is:

$$\text{NPV of C} = \$1,137,236 - \$1,000,000 = \$137,236$$

$$\text{NPV of D} = \$7,160,172 - \$1,000,000 = \$6,160,172$$

Because C and D each have positive net present values, each is
expected to increase the value of the firm. And because D has the
higher NPV, it provides the greater increase in value. If we had to
choose between them, D is much better since it is expected to
increase owners' wealth by over $6 million.

The net present value technique considers all future incremental cash flows. D's NPV with a large cash flow in year 2005 is
much greater than C's NPV.

**Criterion 2: Does Net Present Value Consider the
Timing of Cash Flows?**
Let's look again at projects E and F, whose total cash flow is the
same but whose yearly cash flows differ. The net present values are:

$$\text{NPV of E} = \$1,298,843 - \$1,000,000 = \$298,843$$

$$\text{NPV of F} = \$1,222,301 - \$1,000,000 = \$222,301$$

Both E and F are expected to increase owners' wealth. But E, whose
cash flows are received sooner, has a greater NPV. Therefore, NPV
does consider the timing of the cash flows.

**Criterion 3: Does Net Present Value Consider the
Riskiness of Cash Flows?**
For this we'll look again at investments G and H. They have identical cash flows, although H's inflows are riskier than G's. For G, the
net present value is positive and for H it is negative:

$$\text{NPV of G} = \$1,082,369 - \$1,000,000 = \$82,369$$

$$\text{NPV of H} = \$947,697 - \$1,000,000 = -\$52,303$$

G is acceptable since it is expected to *increase* owners' wealth. H is not acceptable since it is expected to *decrease* owners' wealth. The net present value method is able to distinguish among investments whose cash flows have different risk.

Is Net Present Value Consistent with Owners' Wealth Maximization?

Because the net present value is a measure of how much owners' wealth is expected to increase with an investment, NPV can help us identify projects that maximize owners' wealth.

THE INVESTMENT PROFILE

The net present value technique also allows you to determine the effect of changes in cost of capital on a project's profitability. A project's *investment profile*, also referred to as the *net present value profile*, shows how NPV changes as the discount rate changes. The investment profile is a graphical depiction of the relation between the net present value of a project and the discount rate. It shows the net present value of a project for a range of discount rates.

The net present value profile for Investment A is shown in Exhibit 1 for discount rates from 0% to 40%. To help you get the idea behind this graph, we've identified the NPVs of this project for discount rates of 10% and 20%. The graph shows that the NPV is positive for discount rates from 0% to 28.65% and negative for discount rates higher than 28.65%. Therefore, investment A increases owners' wealth if the cost of capital on this project is less than 28.65% and decreases owners' wealth if the cost of capital on this project is greater than 28.65%.

Let's impose A's NPV profile on the NPV profile of investment B, as shown in Exhibit 2. If A and B are mutually exclusive projects, this graph shows that the project we invest in depends on the discount rate. For higher discount rates, B's NPV falls faster than A's. This is because most of B's present value is attributed to the large cash flows four and five years into the future. The present value of the more distant cash flows is more sensitive to changes in the discount rate than is the present value of cash flows nearer the present.

Exhibit 1: Investment Profile of Investment A

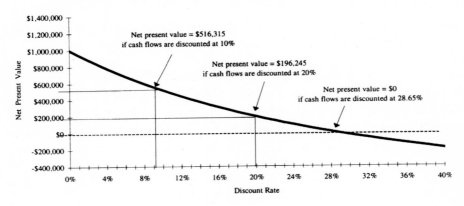

Exhibit 2: Investment Profile of Investments A and B

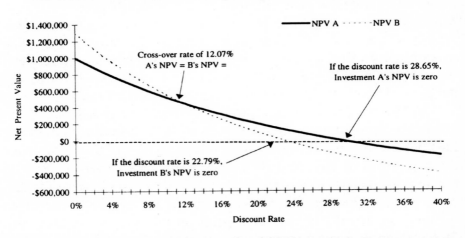

If the discount rate is less than 12.07%, B increases wealth more than A. If the discount rate is more than 12.07% but less than 28.65%, A increases wealth more than B. If the discount rate is greater than 28.65%, we should invest in neither project, since both would decrease wealth. The 12.07% is the *cross-over discount rate* that produces identical NPV's for the two projects. If the discount rate is 12.07%, the net present value of both investments is $1,439,414 – $1,000,000 = $439,414.[1]

NPV AND FURTHER CONSIDERATIONS

The net present value technique considers:

(1) All expected future cash flows
(2) The time value of money
(3) The risk of the future cash flows

Evaluating projects using NPV will lead us to select the ones that maximize owners' wealth. But there are a couple of things we need to take into consideration using net present value.

First, NPV calculations result in a dollar amount, say, $500 or $23,413, which is the incremental value to owners' wealth. However, investors and managers tend to think in terms of percentage returns: Does this project return 10%? 15%?

Second, to calculate NPV we need to know a cost of capital. This is not so easy. The concept behind the cost of capital is simple. It is compensation to the suppliers of capital for (1) the time value of money, and (2) the risk they accept that the cash flows they expect to receive may not materialize as projected. Getting an estimate of how

---

[1] We can solve for the cross-over rate directly. For investments A and B, the cross-over rate is the rate i that equates the net present value of investment A with the net present value of Investment B:

$$-\$1,000,000+\sum_{t}^{5}\frac{\$400,000}{(1+i)^t}=-\$1,000,000+\frac{\$100,000}{(1+i)^1}+\frac{\$100,000}{(1+i)^2}+\frac{\$100,000}{(1+i)^3}+\frac{\$1,000,000}{(1+i)^4}+\frac{\$1,000,000}{(1+i)^5}$$

$$\uparrow \qquad\qquad\qquad\qquad\qquad\qquad\qquad \uparrow$$
$$NPV_A \qquad\qquad\qquad\qquad\qquad\qquad NPV_B$$

Combining like terms — those with the same denominators,

$$\frac{\$400,000-\$100,000}{(1+i)^1}+\frac{\$400,000-\$100,000}{(1+i)^2}+\frac{\$400,000-\$100,000}{(1+i)^3}$$
$$+\frac{\$400,000-\$1,000,000}{(1+i)^4}+\frac{\$400,000-\$1,000,000}{(1+i)^5}=0$$

Simplifying,

$$\frac{\$300,000}{(1+i)^1}+\frac{\$300,000}{(1+i)^2}+\frac{\$300,000}{(1+i)^3}+\frac{-\$600,000}{(1+i)^4}+\frac{-\$600,000}{(1+i)^5}+0$$

This last equation is in the form of a yield problem: the cross-over rate is the rate of return of the *differences* in cash flows of the investments. The i that solves this equation is 12.07%, the cross-over rate.

much compensation is needed is not so simple. That's because to estimate a cost of capital we have to make a judgment on the risk of a project and how much return is needed to compensate for that risk — an issue we address in Section III.

Chapter 6

Profitability Index Technique

The *profitability index* (PI) is the ratio of the present value of change in operating cash inflows to the present value of investment cash outflows:

$$PI = \frac{\text{Present value of the change in operating cash inflows}}{\text{Present value of the investment cash outflows}} \qquad (1)$$

Instead of the *difference* between the two present values, as in the net present value (NPV) calculation, PI is the *ratio* of the two present values. Hence, PI is a variation of NPV. By construction, if the NPV is zero, PI is one.

Suppose the present value of the change in cash inflows is $200,000 and the present value of the change in cash outflows is $200,000. The NPV (the difference between these present values) is zero and the PI (the ratio of these present values) is 1.0.

Looking at investments A and B, the PI for A is:

$$PI \text{ of } A = \frac{\$1,516,315}{\$1,000,000} = 1.5163$$

and the PI of B is:

$$PI \text{ of } B = \frac{\$1,552,620}{\$1,000,000} = 1.5526$$

The PI of 1.5163 means that for each $1 invested in A, we get approximately $1.52 in value; the PI of 1.5526 means that for each $1 invested in B, we get approximately $1.55 in value.

The PI is often referred to as the *benefit-cost ratio*, since it is the ratio of the benefit from an investment (the present value of cash inflows) to its cost (the present value of cash outflows).

PROFITABILITY INDEX DECISION RULE

The profitability index tells us how much value we get for each dollar invested. If the PI is greater than one, we get more than $1 for each $1 invested — if the PI is less than one, we get less than $1 for each $1 invested. Therefore, a project that increases owners' wealth has a PI greater than one.

If ...	this means that ...	and you ...
PI > 1	the investment returns more than $1 in present value for every $1 invested	should accept the project.
PI < 1	the investment returns less than $1 in present value for every $1 invested	should reject the project.
PI = 1	the investment returns $1 in present value for every $1 invested	are indifferent between accepting or rejecting the project.

PROFITABILITY INDEX AS AN EVALUATION TECHNIQUE

How does the profitability index technique stack up against the three criteria? Here's how.

Criterion 1: Does the Profitability Index Consider All Cash Flows?

For investment C,

$$\text{PI of C} = \frac{\$1,137,236}{\$1,000,000} = 1.1372,$$

which indicates that the present value of the change in operating cash flows exceeds the present value investment cash flows. For investment D,

$$\text{PI of D} = \frac{\$7,160,172}{\$1,000,000} = 7.1602,$$

which is much larger than the PI of C, indicating that D produces more value per dollar invested than C.

The PI includes all cash flows.

Criterion 2: Does the Profitability Index Consider the Timing of Cash Flows?

From the data representing investments E and F, which differ on the timing of the future cash flows:

$$\text{PI of E} = \frac{\$1,298,843}{\$1,000,000} = 1.0824 \text{ and PI of F} = \frac{\$1,222,301}{\$1,000,000} = 1.2223$$

The PI of investment E, whose cash flows occur sooner is higher than the PI of F. Hence, the PI considers the time value of money.

Criterion 3: Does the Profitability Index Consider the Riskiness of Cash Flows?

Back again to investments G and H, which have of different risk.

$$\text{PI of G} = \frac{\$1,082,369}{\$1,000,000} = 1.0824 \text{ and PI of H} = \frac{\$947,697}{\$1,000,000} = 0.9477$$

The less risky project, G, has a higher PI and is therefore preferred to H, the riskier project.

The PI is able to distinguish between investment G and the riskier investment, H. The PI of G is greater than the PI of H, even though the expected future cash flows of G and H are the same. The PI does consider the riskiness of the investment's cash flows.

Is the Profitability Index Consistent with Owners' Wealth Maximization?

Rejecting or accepting investments having PI's greater than 1.0 is consistent with rejecting or accepting investments whose NPV is greater than $0. However, in ranking projects, PI might result in one order while NPV might order the same projects differently. This can happen when trying to rank projects that require different amounts to be invested.

Consider the following:

Investment	Present value of cash inflows	Present value of cash outflows	PI	NPV
J	$110,000	$100,000	1.10	$10,000
K	315,000	300,000	1.05	15,000

Investment K has a larger net present value, so it is expected to increase the value of owners' wealth by more than J. But the profitability index values are different: J has a higher PI than K. According to the PI, J is preferred even though it contributes less to the value of the firm. The source of this conflict is the different amounts of investments, that is, scale differences. Because of the way the PI is calculated (as a ratio, instead of a difference), projects that produce the same present value may have different PIs.

Consider two mutually exclusive projects, P and Q:

Project	Present value of inflows	Present value of outflows	PI	NPV
P	$110,000	$100,000	1.10	$10,000
Q	20,000	10,000	2.00	$10,000

If we rank according to the profitability index, project Q is preferred, although they both contribute the same value, $10,000, to the firm.

Consider two mutually exclusive projects, P and R:

Project	Present value of inflows	Present value of outflows	PI	NPV
P	$110,000	$100,000	1.10	$10,000
R	11,000	10,000	1.10	1,000

According to the profitability index, P and R are the same, yet P contributes more value to the firm, $10,000 versus $1,000.

Consider two mutually exclusive projects, P and S:

Project	Present value of inflows	Present value of outflows	PI	NPV
P	$110,000	$100,000	1.10	$10,000
S	120,000	110,000	1.09	10,000

Ranking on the basis of the profitability index, P is preferred to S, even though they contribute the same value to the firm: $10,000.

Seen enough? If the projects are mutually exclusive and have different scales, selecting a project on the basis of the profitability index may not provide the best decision in terms of owners' wealth. As long as we don't have to choose among projects, so that we can take on all profitable projects, using PI produces the same decision as NPV. If the projects are *mutually exclusive* and they are *different scales*, PI cannot be used.

If there is a limit on how much we can spend on capital projects, PI is useful. Limiting the capital budget is referred to as *capital rationing*. Capital rationing limits the amount that can be spent on capital investments during a particular period of time, that is, a limit on the capital budget. These constraints may arise out some policy of the board of directors, or may arise externally, say from creditor agreements that limit capital spending. If a firm has limited management personnel, the board of directors may not want to take on more projects than they feel they can effectively manage.

Consider the following three projects:

Project	Investment	NPV	PI
X	$10,000	$6,000	1.6
Y	$10,000	$5,000	1.5
Z	$20,000	$8,000	1.4

If there is a limit of $20,000 on what we can spend, which project or group of projects are best in terms of maximizing owners' wealth? If we base our choice on NPV, choosing the projects with the highest NPV, we would choose Z, whose NPV is $8,000. If we base our choice on PI, we would choose projects X and Y — those with the highest PI — providing a NPV of $6,000 + 5,000 = $11,000.

Our goal in selecting projects when the capital budget is limited is to select those projects that provide the highest *total NPV*, given our constrained budget. We could use NPV to select projects, but we cannot *rank* projects on the basis of NPV and always get the greatest value for our investment. As an alternative, we could calculate the total NPV for all possible combinations of investments or use a management science technique, such as linear programming, to find the optimal set of project. If we have many projects to choose from, we can also rank projects on the basis of their PIs and choose those projects with the highest PIs that fit into our capital budget.

Selecting projects based on PI, when capital is limited, provides us with the maximum total NPV for our total capital budget. The overriding goal of the firm is to maximize owners' wealth. But if you limit capital spending, the firm may have to forego projects that are expected to increase owners' wealth and therefore owners' wealth is not maximized.

Chapter 7

Internal Rate of Return Technique

Suppose you are offered an investment opportunity that requires you to put up $50,000 and has expected cash inflows of $28,809.52 after one year and $28,809.52 after two years. We can evaluate this opportunity using the following time line:

Today	One year from today	Two years from today
−$50,000.00	$28,809.52	$28,809.52

The return on this investment is the discount rate that causes the present values of the $28,809.52 cash inflows to equal the present value of the $50,000 cash outflow:

$$\$50,000.00 = \frac{\$28,809.52}{(1+i)^1} + \frac{\$28,809.52}{(1+i)^2}$$

Solving for the return i:

$$\$50,000.00 = \$28,809.52 \left[\frac{1}{(1+i)^1} + \frac{1}{(1+i)^2} \right]$$

$$\frac{\$50,000.00}{\$28,809.52} = \left[\frac{1}{(1+i)^1} + \frac{1}{(1+i)^2} \right]$$

$$1.7355 = \left(\begin{array}{c} \text{present value annuity factor} \\ N = 2, i = ? \end{array} \right)$$

The right side is the present value annuity factor, so we can use the tables to determine i, where N is the number of cash flows. Using the present value annuity table or a calculator annuity function, $i = 10\%$. The yield on this investment is therefore 10% per year.

Let's look at this problem from a different angle, so we can see the relation between the net present value and the internal rate of return. Calculate the net present value of this investment at 10% per year:

$$\text{NPV} = -\$50,000.00 + \frac{\$28,809.52}{(1+0.10)^1} + \frac{\$28,809.52}{(1+0.10)^2} = \$0$$

Therefore, the net present value of the investment is zero, when cash flows are discounted at the yield.

INTERNAL RATE OF RETURN CALCULATION

An investment's *internal rate of return* (IRR) is the discount rate that makes the present value of all expected future cash flows equal to zero; or, in other words, the IRR is the discount rate that causes NPV to equal $0.

We can represent the IRR as the rate that solves:

$$\$0 = \sum_{t=1}^{N} \frac{\text{CF}_t}{(1+\text{IRR})^t} \tag{1}$$

Let's return to investments A and B. The IRR for investment A is the discount rate that solves:

$$\$0$$
$$= -\$1,000,000 + \frac{\$400,000}{(1+\text{IRR})^1} + \frac{\$400,000}{(1+\text{IRR})^2} + \frac{\$400,000}{(1+\text{IRR})^3} + \frac{\$400,000}{(1+\text{IRR})^4} + \frac{\$400,000}{(1+\text{IRR})^5}$$

Recognizing that the cash inflows are the same each period and rearranging,

$$\frac{\$1,000,000}{\$400,000} = 1.25$$

Using the present value annuity factor table, we see that the discount rate that solves this equation is approximately 30% per year. Using a calculator or a computer, we get the more precise answer of 28.65% per year.

Let's calculate the IRR for B, so that we can see how we can use IRR to value investments. The IRR for Investment B is the discount rate that solves:

$0

$$= -\$1,000,000 + \frac{\$100,000}{(1+\text{IRR})^1} + \frac{\$100,000}{(1+\text{IRR})^2} + \frac{\$100,000}{(1+\text{IRR})^3} + \frac{\$100,000}{(1+\text{IRR})^4} + \frac{\$100,000}{(1+\text{IRR})^5}$$

Since the cash inflows are not the same amount each period, we cannot use the short-cut of solving for the present value annuity factor, as we did for investment A. We can solve for the IRR of investment B by: (1) trial and error, (2) calculator, or (3) computer.

Trial and error requires a starting point. To make the trial and error a bit easier, let's rearrange the equation, putting the present value of the cash outflows on the left-hand side:

$$\$1,000,000 = \frac{\$100,000}{(1+\text{IRR})^1} + \frac{\$100,000}{(1+\text{IRR})^2} + \frac{\$100,000}{(1+\text{IRR})^3} + \frac{\$100,000}{(1+\text{IRR})^4} + \frac{\$100,000}{(1+\text{IRR})^5}$$

If we try IRR = 10% per year, the right-hand side is greater than the left-hand side:

$$\$1,000,000 \neq \$1,552,620$$

This tells us that we have not discounted enough. Increasing the discount rate to 20% per year,

$$\$1,000,000 \neq \$1,094,779$$

We *still* haven't discounted the cash flows enough. Increasing the discount rate still further, to 25% per year,

$$\$1,000,000 \neq \$932,480$$

We discounted *too* much — we drove the right-hand side below $1,000,000. But at least now we know the IRR is between 20% and 25%. Using a calculator or computer, the precise value of IRR is 22.79% per year.[1]

---

[1] Your calculator does not arrive at the solution directly. Your calculator's program uses trial and error also, and keeps you waiting as it tries different discount rates.

Looking back at Exhibit 1 in Chapter 5, the investment profiles of investments A and B, you'll notice that each profile crosses the horizontal axis (where NPV = $0) at the discount rate that corresponds to the investment's internal rate of return. This is no coincidence: by definition, the IRR is the discount rate that causes the project's NPV to equal zero.

INTERNAL RATE OF RETURN DECISION RULE

The internal rate of return is a yield: what we earn, on average, per year. How do we use it to decide which investment, if any, to choose? Let's revisit investments A and B and the IRRs we just calculated for each. If, for similar risk investments, owners earn 10% per year, then both A and B are attractive. They both yield *more* than the rate owners require for the level of risk of these two investments:

Investment	IRR	Cost of capital
A	28.65% per year	10% per year
B	22.79%	10%

The decision rule for the internal rate of return is to invest in a project if it provides a return greater than the cost of capital. The cost of capital, in the context of the IRR, is a hurdle rate — the minimum acceptable rate of return.

If ...	This means that ...	and you ...
IRR > cost of capital	the investment is expected to return more than required ...	should accept the project.
IRR < cost of capital	the investment is expected to return less than required ...	should reject the project.
IRR = cost of capital	the investment is expected to return what is required ...	are indifferent between accepting or rejecting the project.

The IRR and Mutually Exclusive Projects

What if we were forced to choose *between* projects A and B because they are mutually exclusive? A has a higher IRR than B — so at first glance we might want to accept A. But wait! What about the NPV of A and B? What does the NPV tell us to do?

Investment	IRR	NPV
A	28.65%	$516,315
B	22.79%	$552,620

If we use the higher IRR, it tells us to go with A. If we use the higher NPV, we go with B. Which is correct? If 10% is the cost of capital we used to determine both NPVs and we choose A, we will be foregoing value in the amount of $552,620 − $516,315 = $36,305. Therefore, we should choose B, the one with the higher NPV.

In this example, if for both A and B the cost of capital were different, say 25%, we would calculate different NPVs and come to a different conclusion. In this case:

Investment	IRR	NPV
A	28.65%	$75,712
B	22.79%	−$67,520

Investment A still has a positive NPV, since its IRR > 25%, but B has a negative NPV, since its IRR < 25%.

When evaluating mutually exclusive projects, the one with the highest IRR may not be the one with the best NPV. The IRR may give a different decision than NPV when evaluating mutually exclusive projects because of the reinvestment assumption:

- NPV assumes cash flows are reinvested at the cost of capital.
- IRR assumes cash flows are reinvested at the internal rate of return.

This reinvestment assumption lead to different decisions in choosing among mutually exclusive projects when any of the following factors apply:

- The timing of the cash flows is different among the projects
- There are scale differences (that is, very different cash flow amounts)
- The projects have different useful lives

Let's see the effect of the timing of cash flows in choosing between two projects: investment A's cash flows are received sooner than B's. Part of the return on each investment comes from the reinvestment of its cash inflows. And in the case of A, there is more return from the reinvestment of cash inflows. The question is, "What do you do with the cash inflows when you get them?" We generally assume that if you receive cash inflows, you'll reinvest those cash flows in other assets.

Now we turn to the reinvestment rate assumption in choosing between these projects. Suppose we can reasonably expect to earn only the cost of capital on our investments. Then, for projects with an IRR above the cost of capital, we would be overstating the return on the investment using the IRR. Consider investment A once again. If the best you can do is reinvest each of the $400,000 cash flows at 10%, these cash flows are worth $2,442,040:

Future value of investment A's cash flows each invested at 10%

$$= \$400,000 \left(\begin{array}{c} \text{future value annuity factor} \\ N = 5 \text{ and } i = 10\% \end{array} \right)$$

$$= \$400,000(6.2051) = \$2,442,040$$

Investing $1,000,000 at the end of 2000 produces a value of $2,442,040 at the end of 2005 (cash flows plus the earnings on these cash flows at 10%). This means that if the best you can do is reinvest cash flows at 10%, then you earn not the IRR of 28.65%, but rather 19.55%:

$$
\begin{array}{lll}
\text{FV} & = \text{PV} & (1+i)^n \\
\$2,442,040 & = \$1,000,000 & (1+i)^5 \\
i & = 19.55\% &
\end{array}
$$

If we evaluate projects on the basis of their IRR, we may select one that does not maximize value.

Remember that the NPV calculation assumes reinvestment at the cost of capital. If the reinvestment rate is assumed to be the project's cost of capital, we would evaluate projects on the basis of the NPV and select the one that maximizes owners' wealth.

The IRR and Capital Rationing

What if there is capital rationing? Suppose investments A and B are independent projects. *Independent projects* mean that the acceptance of one does not prevent the acceptance of the other. And suppose the capital budget is limited to $1,000,000. We are therefore forced to choose between A or B. If we select the one with the highest IRR, we choose A. But A is expected to increase wealth *less* than B. Ranking investments on the basis of their IRRs may not maximize wealth.

We can see this dilemma in Exhibit 3 in Chapter 5. The discount rate at which A's NPV is $0.00 — A's IRR — 28.65%, where A's profile crosses the horizontal axis. Likewise, B's IRR is 22.79%. The discount rate at which A's and B's profiles cross is the crossover rate, 12.07%. For discount rates less than 12.07%, B has the higher NPV. For discount rates greater than 12.07%, A has the higher NPV. If you choose A because it has a higher IRR, and if A's cost of capital is more than 12.07%, you have not chosen the project that produces the greatest value.

Suppose you evaluate four independent projects characterized by the following data:

Project	Investment outlay	NPV	IRR
L	$2,000,000	$150,000	23%
M	3,000,000	250,000	22
N	5,000,000	500,000	21
O	10,000,000	1,000,000	20

If there is no capital rationing, you would spend $20,000,000 since all four have positive NPV's. And we would expect owners' wealth to increase by $1,900,000, the sum of the NPVs.

But suppose the capital budget is limited to $10 million. If you select projects on the basis of their IRRs, you would choose projects L, M, and N. But is this optimal in the sense of maximizing owners' wealth? Let's look at the value added from different investment strategies:

	Investment selection	Amount of investment	Total NPV
Selection based on highest IRRs	L, M, and N	$10,000,000	$900,000
Selection based on highest NPVs	O	10,000,000	1,000,000

We can increase the owners' wealth more with project O than with the combined investment in projects L, M, and N. Therefore, when there is capital rationing, selecting investments on the basis of IRR rankings is not consistent with maximizing wealth.

The source of the problem in the case of capital rationing is that the IRR is a percentage, not a dollar amount. Because of this, we cannot determine how to distribute the capital budget to maximize wealth because the investment or group of investments producing the highest yield does not mean they are the ones that produce the greatest wealth.

INTERNAL RATE OF RETURN AS AN EVALUATION TECHNIQUE

Here is how the internal rate of return technique stacks up against the three criteria.

Criterion 1: Does IRR Consider All Cash Flows?

Looking at investments C and D, the difference between them is D's cash flow in the last year. The internal rate of return for C is 15.24% per year and for D the IRR is 73.46% per year. The IRR considers all cash flows and, as a result, D's IRR is much larger than C's due to the cash flow in the last period.

Criterion 2: Does IRR Consider the Timing of Cash Flows?

To see if the IRR can distinguish investments whose cash flows have different time values of money, let's look at investments E and F. The IRR of E is 15.24% per year.

Notice that investments C and E have identical cash flows, but C's cost of capital is 10% per year and E's cost of capital is 5% per year. Do the different costs of capital affect the calculation of net present value? Yes, since cash flows for C and E are discounted at different rates. Does this affect the calculation of the internal rate of return? No, since we are solving for the discount rate — we do not use the cost of capital. The cost of capital comes into play in making a decision, comparing IRR with the cost of capital.

The IRR of F is 10.15%. Investment E, whose cash flows are received sooner, has a higher IRR than F. The IRR does consider the timing of cash flows.

Criterion 3: Does IRR Consider the Riskiness of Cash Flows?

To examine whether the IRR considers the riskiness of cash flows, let's compare investments G and H. The IRR for G is 7.93%. The cash flows of H are the same as those of G, so its IRR is the same, 7.93% per year.

The IRR of G exceeds the cost of capital, 5% per year, so we would accept G. The IRR of H is less than its cost of capital, 10% per year, so we would reject H. So how does the IRR method consider risk? The calculation of IRR doesn't consider risk, but when we compare a project's IRR with its cost of capital — that is, applying the decision rule — we do consider the risk of the cash flows.

Is IRR Consistent with Owners' Wealth Maximization?
Evaluating projects with IRR indicates the ones that maximize wealth so long as: (1) the projects are independent, and (2) they are not limited by capital rationing. For mutually exclusive projects or capital rationing, the IRR may (but not always) lead to projects that do not maximize wealth.

MULTIPLE INTERNAL RATES OF RETURN

The typical project usually involves only one large negative cash flow initially, followed by a series of future positive flows. But that's not always the case. Suppose you are involved in a project that uses environmentally sensitive chemicals. It may cost you a great deal to dispose of them, which will cause a negative cash flow at the end of the project.

Suppose we are considering a project that has cash flows as follows:

Period	End-of-period cash flow
0	−$100
1	+$474
2	−$400

What is the internal rate of return on this project? Solving for the internal rate of return:

$$\$0 = -\$100 + \frac{\$474}{(1 + \text{IRR})^1} + \frac{-\$400}{(1 + \text{IRR})^2}$$

One possible solution is IRR = 10%. Yet *another* possible solution is IRR = 2.65, or 265%. Therefore, there are two possible solutions, IRR = 10% per year and IRR = 265% per year.

Exhibit 1: Investment Profile of a Project with an Initial Cash Outlay of $100, a First Period Cash Inflow of $474 and a Second Period Cash Outflow of $400, Resulting in Multiple Internal Rates of Return

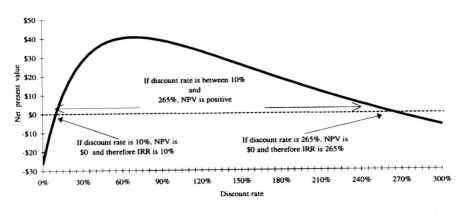

We can see this graphically in Exhibit 1, where the NPV of these cash flows are shown for discount rates from 0% to 300%. Remember that the IRR is the discount rate that causes the NPV to be zero. In terms of this graph, this means that the IRR is the discount rate where the NPV is $0, the point at which the present value changes sign — from positive to negative or from negative to positive. In the case of this project, the present value changes from negative to positive at 10% and from positive to negative at 265%.

Multiple solutions to the yield on a series of cash flows occurs whenever there is more than one change from + to − or from − to + in the sequence of cash flows. For example, the cash flows in the example above followed a pattern of − + −. There are two sign changes: from minus to plus and from plus to minus. There are also two possible solutions for IRR, one for each sign change.

If you end up with multiple solutions, what do you do? Can you use any of these? None of these? If there are multiple solutions, there is no unique internal rate of return. And if there is no unique solution, the solutions we get are worthless as far as making a decision based on IRR. This is a strike against the IRR as an evaluation technique.

Chapter 8

Modified Internal Rate of Return Technique

The *modified internal rate of return* technique is similar to the IRR but uses a more realistic reinvestment assumption. As we saw in the previous chapter, there are situations in which it's not appropriate to use the IRR.

MODIFIED INTERNAL RATE OF RETURN TECHNIQUE

Let's look again at A's IRR of 28.65% per year. This means that, when the first $400,000 comes into the firm, it is reinvested at 28.65% per year for four more periods, when the second $400,000 comes into the firm, it is reinvested at 28.65% per year for three more periods, and so on. If you reinvested all of A's cash inflows at the IRR of 28.65% (that is, you had other investments with the same 28.65% yield) you would have by the end of the project:

End of year	Cash inflow		Value at the end of the project
2001	$400,000	$400,000 $(1 + 0.2865)^4 =$	$1,095,719
2002	400,000	$400,000 $(1 + 0.2865)^3 =$	$851,705
2003	400,000	$400,000 $(1 + 0.2865)^2 =$	$662,033
2004	400,000	$400,000 $(1 + 0.2865)^1 =$	$514,600
2005	400,000	$400,000 $(1 + 0.2865)^0 =$	$400,000
			$3,524,057

Investing $1,000,000 in A contributes $3,524,057 to the future value of the firm in the fifth year, providing a return on the investment of 28.65% per year. Let FV = $3,524,057, PV = $1,000,000, and $n = 5$. Using the basic valuation equation

$$FV = PV(1 + i)^n$$

and substituting the known values for FV, PV, and n, and the r, the IRR is,

$$\$3,524,057 = \$1,000,000(1 + i)^5$$

$$i = 28.65\% \text{ per year}$$

Therefore, by using financial math to solve for the annual return, i, we have assumed that the cash inflows are reinvested at the IRR.

Assuming that cash inflows are reinvested at the IRR is "strike two" against IRR as an evaluation technique if it is an unrealistic rate. One way to get around this problem is to modify the reinvestment rate built into the mathematics.

Suppose you have an investment with the following expected cash flows:

Year	End-of-year cash flow
0	−$10,000
1	+$3,000
2	+$3,000
3	+$6,000

The IRR of this project is 8.55% per year. This IRR assumes you can reinvest each of the inflows at 8.55% per year. To see this, consider what you would have at the end of the third year if you reinvested each cash flow at 8.55%:

Year	End-of-year cash flow	Future value at end of third year, using 8.55%
1	+$3,000	$\$3,000 (1 + 0.0855)^2 = \$3,534.93$
2	+$3,000	$\$3,000 (1 + 0.0855)^1 = \$3,256.50$
3	+$6,000	$\$6,000 (1 + 0.0855)^0 = \$6,000.00$
FV_3		$12,791.43

Investing $10,000 today produces a value of $12,791.43 at the end of the third year. The return on this investment is calculated using the present value of the investment (the $10,000), the future value of the investment (the $12,791.43) and the number of periods (3 in this case):

$$\text{Return on investment} = \sqrt[3]{\frac{\$12,791.43}{\$10,000.00}} - 1 = 8.55\%$$

Let's see what happens when we change the reinvestment assumption. If you invest in this project and each time you receive a cash inflow you stuff it under your mattress, you accumulate $12,000 by the end of the third year: $3,000 + 3,000 + 6,000 = $12,000. What return do you earn on your investment of $10,000?

You invest $10,000 and end up with $12,000 after three years. The $12,000 is the future value of the investment, which is also referred to as the investment's *terminal value*.

We solve for the return on the investment by inserting the known values (PV = $10,000, FV = $12,000, $n = 3$) into the basic valuation equation and solving for the discount rate, i:

$$\$12,000 = \$10,000(1 + i)^3$$

$$(1 + i)^3 = \$12,000/\$10,000$$

$$(1 + i) = \sqrt[3]{1.2} = 1.0627$$

$$i = 0.0627, \text{ or } 6.27\% \text{ per year}$$

The return from this investment, with no reinvestment of cash flows, is 6.27%. We refer to this return as a *modified internal rate of return* (MIRR) because we have *modified* the reinvestment assumption. In this case, we modified the reinvestment rate from the IRR of 8.55% to 0%.

But what if, instead, you could invest the cash inflows in an investment that provides an annual return of 5%? Each cash flow earns 5% annually compounded interest until the end of the third period. We can represent this problem in a time line, shown in Exhibit 1. The future value of the cash inflows, with reinvestment at 5% annually, is:

$$FV = \$3,000 (1 + 0.05)^2 + \$3,000 (1 + 0.05)^1 + \$6,000$$
$$= \$3,307.50 + \$3,150.00 + \$6,000 = \$12,457.50$$

The MIRR is the return on the investment of $10,000 that produces $12,457.50 in three years:

$$\$12,457.50 = \$10,000 (1 + MIRR)^3$$

$$MIRR = 0.0760, \text{ or } 7.60\% \text{ per year.}$$

A way to think about the modified return is to consider breaking down the return into its two components:

1. the return you get if there is no reinvestment (our mattress stuffing)
2. the return from reinvestment of the cash inflows

Exhibit 1: Modified Internal Rate of Return

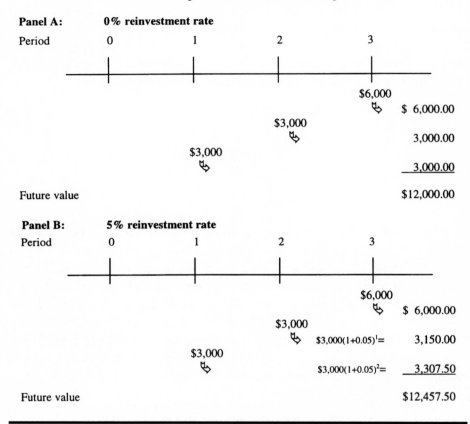

Panel A: **0% reinvestment rate**

Period	0	1	2	3	
				$6,000	$ 6,000.00
			$3,000		3,000.00
		$3,000			3,000.00
Future value					$12,000.00

Panel B: **5% reinvestment rate**

Period	0	1	2	3		
				$6,000		$ 6,000.00
			$3,000		$3,000(1+0.05)^1=	3,150.00
		$3,000			$3,000(1+0.05)^2=	3,307.50
Future value						$12,457.50

We can also represent MIRR in terms of a formula that combines terms we are already familiar with. Consider the three steps in the calculation of MIRR:

> *Step 1:* Calculate the present value of all cash outflows, using the reinvestment rate as the discount rate
>
> *Step 2:* Calculate the future value of all cash inflows reinvested at some rate
>
> *Step 3:* Solve for rate — the MIRR — that causes future value of cash inflows to equal present value of outflows

In this last example,

Reinvestment rate	Modified internal rate of return (MIRR)
0.00%	6.27%
5.00%	7.60%
8.55%	8.55%

If instead of reinvesting each cash flow at 0%, we reinvest at 5% per year, then the reinvestment adds 7.60% − 6.27% = 1.33% to the investment's return. But wait — we reinvested at 5%. Why doesn't reinvestment add 5%? Because you only earn on reinvestment of intermediate cash flows (the first $3,000 for two periods at 5% and the second $3,000 for one period at 5%) not all cash flows.

Let's calculate the MIRR for investments A and B, assuming reinvestment at the 10% cost of capital.

Step 1: Calculate the present value of the cash outflows. In both A's and B's case, this is $1,000,000.

Step 2: Calculate the future value by figuring the future value of each cash flow as of the end of 2005:[1]

Year	Investment A		Investment B	
	End-of-year cash flows	End-of-year 2005 value of cash flow	End-of-year cash flow	End-of-year 2005 value of cash flow
2001	$400,000	$585,640	$100,000	$146,410
2002	400,000	532,400	100,000	133,100
2003	400,000	484,000	100,000	121,100
2004	400,000	440,000	1,000,000	1,100,000
2005	400,000	400,000	1,000,000	1,100,000
Future value		$2,442,040		$2,500,510

Step 3: For A, solve for the rate that equates $2,442,040 in five years with $1,000,000 today:

$$\$2,442,040 = \$1,000,000 \, (1 + MIRR)^5$$

$$MIRR = 0.1955 \text{ or } 19.55\% \text{ per year}$$

Following the same steps, the MIRR for investment B is 20.12% per year.

---

[1] We have taken each cash flow and determined its value at the end of the year 2005. We could cut down our work by recognizing that these cash inflows are even amounts — simplifying the first step to the calculation of the future value of an ordinary annuity.

MODIFIED INTERNAL RATE OF RETURN DECISION RULE

The modified internal rate of return is a return on the investment, assuming a particular return on the reinvestment of cash flows. As long as the MIRR is greater than the cost of capital (that is, MIRR > cost of capital) the project should be accepted. If the MIRR is less than the cost of capital, the project does not provide a return commensurate with the amount of risk of the project.

If ...	this means that	and you ...
MIRR > cost of capital	the investment is expected to return more than required	should accept the project.
MIRR < cost of capital	the investment is expected to return less than required	should reject the project.
MIRR = cost of capital	the investment is expected to return what is required	are indifferent between accepting or rejecting the project

Consider Investments A and B and their MIRRs with reinvestment at the cost of capital:

Investment	MIRR	IRR	NPV
A	19.55%	28.65%	$516,315
B	20.12%	22.79%	$552,619

Assume for now that these are mutually exclusive investments. We saw the danger trying to rank projects on their IRRs if the projects are mutually exclusive. But what if we ranked projects according to MIRR? In this example, there seems to be a correspondence between MIRR and NPV. In the case of investments A and B, MIRR and NPV provide identical rankings.

MODIFIED INTERNAL RATE OF RETURN AS AN EVALUATION TECHNIQUE

Now we'll go through our usual drill of assessing this technique according to the three criteria.

Criterion 1: Does MIRR Consider All Cash Flows?

Assume the cash inflows from investments C and D are reinvested at the cost of capital of 10% per year. We find that the modified internal rate of return for C is 12.87% per year and for D is 63.07% per year.[2] D's larger cash flow in year 2005 is reflected in the larger MIRR. MIRR does consider all cash flows.

Criterion 2: Does MIRR Consider the Timing of Cash Flows?

To see whether the MIRR can distinguish investments whose cash flows occur at different points in time, calculate the MIRR for investments E and F. Using the terminal values for E and F of $1,831,530 and $1,620,000, respectively, we solve for the rate that equates the terminal value in five years with each investment's $1,000,000 outlay. The MIRR of E is 12.87% per year and the MIRR of F is 10.13% per year. E's cash flows are expected sooner than F's. This is reflected in the higher MIRR. Both E and F are acceptable investments because they provide a return above the cost of capital. If we had to choose between E and F, we would choose E because it has a higher MIRR. MIRR does consider the timing of cash flows.

Criterion 3: Does MIRR Consider the Riskiness of Cash Flows?

Let's look at the MIRR for investments G and H, which have identical expected cash flows, although H's inflows are riskier. Assuming that cash flows are reinvested at the 5% per year cost of capital for G and 10% per year for H, the future values are $1,381,408 and $1,526,275, respectively. The MIRR for G is 6.68%, calculated using the investment of $1,000,000 as the present value and the terminal value of $1,381,408. Using the same procedure, the MIRR for H is 8.82% per year. Comparing the MIRRs with the costs of capital.

Investment	MIRR	Cost of capital	Decision
G	6.68%	5%	Accept
H	8.82%	10%	Reject

If we reinvest cash flows at the cost of capital and if the costs of capital are different, we get different terminal values and hence different MIRRs for G and H. If we then compare each project's MIRR with the project's cost of capital, we can determine the projects that would increase owners' wealth.

---

[2] The terminal values for C and D are $1,831,530 and $11,531,530, respectively.

MIRR distinguishes between the investments, but choosing the investment with the highest MIRR may not give the value maximizing decision. In the case of G and H, H has a higher MIRR. But, when each project's MIRR is compared to the cost of capital, we see that investment H should not be accepted. This points out the danger of using MIRR when capital is rationed or when choosing among mutually exclusive projects: ranking and selecting projects on the basis of their MIRR may lead to a decision that does not maximize owners' wealth. If projects are not independent, or if capital is rationed, we are faced with some of the same problems we encountered with the IRR in those situations: MIRR may not produce the decision that maximizes owners' wealth.

Is MIRR Consistent with Owners' Wealth Maximization?

MIRR can be used to evaluate whether to invest in independent projects and identify the ones that maximize owners' wealth. However, decisions made using MIRR are not consistent with maximizing wealth when selecting among mutually exclusive projects or when there is capital rationing.

Chapter 9

Comparing Evaluation Techniques and Some Concluding Thoughts

T he results of our calculations using the six techniques we have discussed are summarized in Exhibit 1. If each of the eight projects are independent and are not limited by capital rationing, all projects except investment H are expected to increase owners' wealth.

Suppose each project is independent, yet we have a capital budget limit of $5 million on the total amount we can invest. Since each of the eight projects requires $1 million, we can only invest in five of them. Which five projects do we invest in? In order of NPV, we choose: D, B, A, E, and F. We would expect the value of owners' wealth to increase by $6,160,172 + 552,620 + 516,315 + 298,843 + 222,301 = $7,750,251.

Now suppose that each pair of projects is a set of mutually exclusive projects. Which project of each mutually exclusive pair is preferred? Investments B, D, E, and G are preferred, choosing the projects with the higher NPV of each pair.

Exhibit 1: Summary of the Evaluation of the Investment Projects

Investment	Required rate of return	Payback period	Discounted payback period	Net present value	Profitability index	Internal rate of return	Modified internal rate of return
A	10%	3 years	4 years	$516,315	1.5163	28.65%	19.55%
B	10%	4 years	5 years	552,620	1.5526	22.79%	20.12%
C	10%	4 years	4 years	137,236	1.1372	15.24%	12.87%
D	10%	4 years	4 years	6,160,172	7.1602	73.46%	63.07%
E	5%	4 years	4 years	298,843	1.2988	15.24%	12.87%
F	5%	4 years	5 years	222,301	1.2223	10.15%	10.13%
G	5%	4 years	5 years	82,369	1.0823	7.93%	6.68%
H	10%	4 years	not paid back	−52,303	0.9477	7.93%	8.82%

If you are considering mutually exclusive projects, the NPV method leads us to invest in projects that maximize wealth. If your capital budget is limited, the NPV and PI methods lead us to the set of projects that maximize wealth.

SCALE DIFFERENCES

Scale differences (differences in the amount of the cash flows) between projects can lead to conflicting investment decisions among the discounted cash flow techniques. Consider two projects, Project Big and Project Little, that each have a cost of capital of 5% per year with the following cash flows:

End of Period	Project Big	Project Little
0	-$1,000,000	-$1.00
1	+400,000	+0.40
2	+400,000	+0.40
3	+400,000	+0.50

Applying the discounted cash flow techniques to each project,

Discounted Cash Flow Technique	Project Big	Project Little
NPV	$89,299	$0.1757
PI	1.0893	1.1757
IRR	9.7010%	13.7789%
MIRR	8.0368%	10.8203%

Mutually Exclusive Projects

If Big and Little are mutually exclusive projects, which project should a firm prefer? If the firm goes strictly by the PI, IRR, or MIRR criteria, it would choose Project Little. But is this the better project? Project Big provides more value: $89,299 versus 18¢. The techniques that ignore the scale of the investment — PI, IRR, and MIRR — may lead to an incorrect decision.

Capital Rationing

If the firm is subject to capital rationing (say, a limit of $1 million) and Big and Little are independent projects, which project should the firm choose? The firm can only choose one — spend $1 or $1,000,000, but not $1,000,001. If you go strictly by the PI, IRR, or

MIRR criteria, the firm would choose Project Little. But is this the better project? Again, the techniques that ignore the scale of the investment — PI, IRR, and MIRR — lead to an incorrect decision.

CHOOSING THE APPROPRIATE TECHNIQUE

The advantages and disadvantages of each of the techniques for evaluating investments are summarized in Exhibit 2. We see in this chart that the discounted cash flow techniques are preferred to the nondiscounted cash flow techniques. The discounted cash flow techniques — NPV, PI, IRR, MIRR — are preferable since they consider (1) all cash flows, (2) the time value of money, and (3) the risk of future cash flows. The discounted cash flow techniques are also useful because we can apply objective decision criteria, criteria we can actually use that tells us when a project increases wealth and when it does not.

We also see in Exhibit 2 that not all of the discounted cash flow techniques are right for every situation. There are questions we need to ask when evaluating an investment and the answers will determine which technique is the one to use for that investment:

- Are the projects mutually exclusive or independent?
- Are the projects subject to capital rationing?
- Are the projects of the same risk?
- Are the projects of the same scale of investment?

If projects are independent and not subject to capital rationing, we can evaluate them and determine the ones that maximize wealth based on any of the discounted cash flow techniques. If the projects are mutually exclusive, have the same investment outlay, and have the same risk, we must use only the NPV or the MIRR techniques to determine the projects that maximize wealth. If projects are mutually exclusive and are of different risks or are of different scales, NPV is preferred over MIRR. If the capital budget is limited, we can use either the NPV or the PI. We must be careful, however, not to select projects on the basis of their NPV (that is, ranking on NPV and selecting the highest NPV projects) but rather how we can maximize the NPV of the total capital budget.

Exhibit 2: Summary of Characteristics of the Evaluation Techniques

PAYBACK PERIOD

Advantages	Disadvantages
[1] Simple to compute. [2] Provides some information on the risk of the investment. [3] Provides a crude measure of liquidity.	[1] No concrete decision criteria to tell us whether an investment increases the firm's value. [2] Ignores cash flows beyond the payback period. [3] Ignores the time value of money. [4] Ignores the riskiness of future cash flows.

DISCOUNTED PAYBACK PERIOD

Advantages	Disadvantages
[1] Considers the time value of money. [2] Considers the riskiness of the cash flows involved in the payback.	[1] No concrete decision criteria that tell us whether the investment increases the firm's value. [2] Calls for a cost of capital. [3] Ignores cash flows beyond the payback period.

NET PRESENT VALUE

Advantages	Disadvantages
[1] Decision criteria that tell us whether the investment will increase the firm's value. [2] Considers all cash flows. [3] Considers the time value of money. [4] Considers the riskiness of future cash flows.	[1] Requires a cost of capital for calculation. [2] Expressed in terms of dollars, not as a percentage.

PROFITABILITY INDEX

Advantages	Disadvantages
[1] Decision criteria that tell us whether an investment increases the firm's value. [2] Considers all cash flows. [3] Considers the time value of money. [4] Considers the riskiness of future cash flows. [5] Useful in ranking and selecting projects when capital is rationed.	[1] Requires a cost of capital for calculation. [2] May not give correct decision when comparing mutually exclusive projects.

INTERNAL RATE OF RETURN

Advantages	Disadvantages
[1] Decision criteria that tell us whether an investment increases the firm's value. [2] Considers the time value of money. [3] Considers all cash flows. [4] Consider riskiness of future cash flows.	[1] Requires a cost of capital for decision. [2] May not give value maximizing decision when comparing mutually exclusive projects. [3] May not give value maximizing decision when choosing projects with capital rationing.

MODIFIED INTERNAL RATE OF RETURN

Advantages	Disadvantages
[1] Decision criteria that tell us whether the investment increases the firm's value. [2] Considers the time value of money. [3] Considers all cash flows. [4] Consider riskiness of future cash flows.	[1] May not give value maximizing decision when comparing mutually exclusive projects with different scales or different risk. [2] May not give value maximizing decision when choosing projects with capital rationing.

CAPITAL BUDGETING TECHNIQUES IN PRACTICE

Among the evaluation techniques in this chapter, the one we can be sure about is the net present value method. NPV will steer us toward the project that maximizes wealth in the most general circumstances. But what evaluation technique do financial decision makers really use?

We learn about what goes on in practice by anecdotal evidence and through surveys. These indicate that:

- There is an increased use of more sophisticated capital budgeting techniques.
- Most financial managers use more than one technique to evaluate the same projects, with a discounted cash flow technique (NPV, IRR, PI) used as a primary method and payback period used as a secondary method.
- The most commonly used is the internal rate of return method, though the net present value method is gaining acceptance.
- There is evidence that firms use hurdle rates (that is, costs of capital) that are higher than most cost of capital techniques would suggest.

The IRR is popular most likely because it is a measure of yield and therefore easy to understand. Moreover, since NPV is expressed in dollars, the expected increment in the value of the firm and financial managers are accustomed to dealing with yields, they may be more comfortable dealing with the IRR than the NPV.

The popularity of the IRR method is troublesome since it may lead to decisions about projects that are not in the best interest of owners. However, the NPV method is becoming more widely accepted and, in time, may replace the IRR as the more popular method.

Is the use of payback period troublesome? Not necessarily. The payback period is generally used as a screening device, eliminating those projects that cannot even break even. Further, the payback period can be viewed as a measure of a yield. If the future cash flows are the same amount each period and if these future cash flows can be assumed to be received each period forever — essentially, a perpetuity — then the reciprocal of the payback period is a rough guide to a yield on the investment. Suppose you invest $100 today and expect $20 each period, forever. The payback period is five years. The inverse, $\frac{1}{5} = 20\%$ per year, is the yield on the investment.

Now let's turn this relation around and create a payback period rule. Suppose we want a 10% per year return on our investment. This means that the payback period should be less than, or equal to, 10 years. So, while the payback period may seem to be a rough guide, there is some rationale behind it.

Use of the simpler techniques, such as payback period, does not mean that a firm has unsophisticated capital budgeting. Remember that evaluating the cash flows is only one aspect of the process:

- Cash flows must first be estimated.
- Cash flows are evaluated using NPV, PI, IRR, MIRR, or a payback method.
- Project risk must be assessed to determine the cost of capital.

Conflicts with Responsibility Center Performance Evaluation Measures

There are various measures used by corporations to evaluate the performance of managers of divisions and departments. Two commonly used measures are return on investment (ROI) and residual income. It is possible for a proposed project to be attractive based on the techniques we discussed in Section II, but a manager may reject it because the project would adversely impact the performance measure used by the firm to evaluate his or her performance.

For example, suppose that a division manager is considering two mutually exclusive projects. The first is a project with an expected life of five years and requires a cash outlay in the initial year. The other is a project with an expected life of 10 years and requires a larger investment outlay. The outlay will be made in the initial year and the following two years. Suppose further that, using all the project evaluation techniques, the second project is clearly superior to the first project. But the second project might typically have an adverse impact on the manager's performance in the first and second years compared to the first project. Thus, the manager may bias his or her decision toward accepting the less attractive project.

As a result, while the techniques we discuss in Section II for evaluating investment proposals are sound, the measures employed to evaluate managers may bias their decisions against the selection of the best projects. The goal is to establish measures to evaluate the performance of managers that are consistent with the project evaluation techniques discussed in the chapters in this section of the book.

CAPITAL BUDGETING AND THE JUSTIFICATION OF NEW TECHNOLOGY

You now have all the tools to evaluate a capital budgeting proposal. Although the "mechanics" of calculating the profitability measures given (1) the initial cash flows, (2) the cash flow from operations, and (3) the required return (or hurdle rate) are not complicated, remember what we warned you about in Section I. The most complex stage of the capital budgeting procedure is estimating cash flows.

An army of analysts equipped with the tools described in Section II have marched out of universities ready to apply these techniques in U.S. firms. However, informed observers have felt that these tools have not been properly utilized.[1] More specifically, informed observers have cited examples where the capital budgeting techniques that we have discussed have failed to recognize the potential profitability of acquiring new technological equipment.

When new technological equipment, such as a newly created computer-aided production process, is considered for acquisition, the cash flows must be estimated. Does management do a good job of estimating the potential benefits from such technologies? Informed observers do not believe they do. For example, in a survey conducted as part of a Boston University Roundtable, 78% of the respondents felt that:[2]

> ... most businesses in the U.S. will remain so tied to traditional quantitative investment criteria that they

---

[1] See, for example, Robert H. Hayes and David A. Garvin, "Managing as if Tomorrow Mattered," Harvard *Business Review* (May-June 1982).

[2] As cited in Robert S. Kaplan and Anthony A. Atkinson, *Advanced Management Accounting* (Englewood Cliffs, New Jersey: Prentice-Hall, 1989): 474.

will be unable to properly evaluate the potential value
of computer-aided manufacturing options.

It is believed, and has been observed, that those making capital budgeting decisions fail to (or refuse to) take into consideration
critical factors that may improve future cash flow as a result of the
introduction of a new technology. Remember, we are not simply
talking about replacing one type of equipment with a slightly technologically superior one. Rather, our focus here is on new technologies that will significantly alter the production process. Not only is
the impact on the future cost structure of the firm important, but the
potential impact on its competitive position — domestic and global
— must be assessed.

Underestimating the potential benefits when projecting cash
flows results in a bias in favor of rejecting a new technology. But
there are more problems. The estimated cash flows must be discounted. In the experience of the authors, it is not uncommon for
firms to select a very high after-tax required return to evaluate new
technologies. Of course, there is nothing wrong with using a high
after-tax required return if financial analysis demonstrates that such
a return is warranted. The proper analysis of risk is a topic that is
discussed Section III. However, for some firms the analysis underlying the setting of a high required rate ranges from little to none;
or, put another way, for some firms the high required rate is arbitrarily determined. Even when there is analysis performed to determine the appropriate required return, the calculation may be based
incorrectly on a financial accounting measure, such as return to
stockholders' equity that may be some high rate.

Why does a high required return (or equivalently, discount
rate) bias the acceptance of new technologies? Recall our old friend
the time-value of money. We know that the further into the future the
positive cash flows, the lower will be all of the discounted flow measures we described. We also know that the higher the discount rate
the lower the NPV and profitability index. (In the case of the IRR, it
will have to exceed the high discount rate.) Now consider a typical
new technology that is being considered by a firm. It may take one or
more years to get the new technology up and running. Consequently,

positive cash flow may not be seen for several years. A high discount rate coupled with positive cash flows not coming in for several years will bias the decision in the direction of rejecting a new technology. For example, suppose a discount rate of 22% is required on a project and that a positive cash flow is not realized for at least four years. Then the present value of a positive cash flow of $1 four years from now at 22% is $0.45; for a positive cash flow of $1 ten years from now, the present value is $0.14. On the other hand, if the correct discount rate is, say, 13%, then the present value of a $1 positive cash flow would be $0.61 if it received four years from now and $0.29 if it is received ten years from now. You can see the dramatic impact of an unwarranted high discount rate. Add to this the underestimation of the positive cash flows by not properly capturing all the benefits from the introduction of a new technology and you can see why U.S. firms have been reluctant to acquire new technologies using "state-of-the-art" capital budgeting techniques. Is it any wonder that respondents to a study conducted by the Automation Forum found that the financial justification of automated equipment was the number on impediment to its introduction into U.S. firms.[3]

All of this is not to say that the capital budgeting techniques described in this book should not be used to analyze whether to acquire new technologies. Quite the contrary. We believe that, *if properly employed* — that is, good cash flow estimation capturing all the benefits that can be realized from introducing a new technology, and the proper calculation of a discount rate — they can help identify opportunities available from new technologies.

---

[3] Sandra B. Dornan, "Justifying New Technologies," *Production* (July 1987).

Case for Section II

NASTY-AS-CAN-BE CANDY

National Foods is considering producing a new candy, Nasty-As-Can-Be. National has spent two years and $450,000 developing this product. National has also test marketed Nasty, spending $100,000 to conduct consumer surveys and tests of the product in 25 states.

Based on previous candy products and the results in the test marketing, management believes consumers will buy 4 million packages each year for ten years at 50 cents per package. Equipment to produce Nasty will cost National $1,000,000, and $300,000 of additional net working capital will be required to support Nasty sales. National expects production costs to average 60% of Nasty's net revenues, with overhead and sales expenses totaling $525,000 per year. The equipment has a life of ten years, after which time it will have no salvage value. Working capital is assumed to be fully recovered at the end of ten years. Depreciation is straight-line (no salvage) and National's tax rate is 45%. The required rate of return for projects of similar risk is 8%.

Requirements

a. Should National Foods produce this new candy? What is the basis of your recommendation?

b. Would your recommendation change if production costs average 65% of net revenues instead of 60%? How sensitive is your recommendation to production costs?

c. Would your recommendation change if the equipment were depreciated according to MACRS as a 10-year asset instead of using straight-line?

d. Suppose that competitors are expected to introduce similar candy products to compete with Nasty, such that dollar sales will drop by 5% each year following the first-year. Should National Foods produce this new candy considering this possible drop in sales? Explain.

Questions for Section II

1. What is the objective of evaluating investments?

2. What criteria must be satisfied for an investment evaluation technique to be ideal?

3. Distinguish between the payback period and the discounted payback period.

4. In our examples using the payback period and discounted payback period, we end up with a payback period in terms of a whole number of periods instead of a fractional number of periods. Why?

5. Why is it that, when the post-payback duration is zero, the investment is not profitable and should be rejected without further analysis?

6. Can the payback period method of evaluating projects identify the ones that will maximize wealth? Explain.

7. Can the discounted payback period method of evaluating projects identify the ones that will maximize wealth? Explain.

8. Consider two projects, AA and BB, that have identical, positive net present values, but Project BB is riskier than AA. If these projects are mutually exclusive, what is your investment decision?

9. Can the net present value method of evaluating projects identify the ones that will maximize wealth? Explain.

10. The decision rules for the net present value and the profitability index methods are related. Explain the relationship between these two sets of decision rules.

11. What is the source of the conflict between net present value and the profitability index decision rules in evaluating mutually exclusive projects.

12. Suppose you calculate a project's net present value to be $3,000. What does this mean?

13. Suppose you calculate a project's profitability index to be 1.4. What does this mean?

14. The internal rate of return is often referred to as the *yield on an investment*. Explain the analogy between the internal rate of return on an investment and the yield to maturity on a bond.

15. The net present value method and the internal rate of return method may produce different decisions when selecting among mutually exclusive projects. What is the source of this conflict?

16. The net present value method and the internal rate of return method may produce different decisions when selecting projects under capital rationing. What is the source of this conflict?

17. The modified internal rate of return is designed to overcome a deficiency in the internal rate of return method. Specifically, what problem is the MIRR designed to overcome?

18. Based upon our analysis of the alternative techniques to evaluate projects, which method or methods are preferable in terms of maximizing owners' wealth?

19. Based upon studies of capital project evaluation in practice, which method or methods are preferred by those actually using these techniques?

20. Why do we find a gap between what is preferred in terms of owners' wealth maximization, and what is used in practice for capital project evaluation?

Problems for Section II

1. You are evaluating an investment project, Project ZZ, with the following cash flows:

Period	Cash flow
0	−$100,000
1	35,027
2	35,027
3	35,027
4	35,027

Calculate the following:
(a) Payback period
(b) Discounted payback period, assuming a 10% cost of capital
(c) Discounted payback period, assuming a 16% cost of capital
(d) Net present value, assuming a 10% cost of capital
(e) Net present value, assuming a 16% cost of capital
(f) Profitability index, assuming a 10% cost of capital
(g) Profitability index, assuming a 16% cost of capital
(h) Internal rate of return
(i) Modified internal rate of return, assuming reinvestment at 0%
(j) Modified internal rate of return, assuming reinvestment at 10%

2. You are evaluating an investment project, Project YY, with the following cash flows:

Period	Cash flow
0	−$100,000
1	43,798
2	43,798
3	43,798

Calculate the following:
(a) Payback period
(b) Discounted payback period, assuming a 10% cost of capital
(c) Discounted payback period, assuming a 14% cost of capital
(d) Net present value, assuming a 10% cost of capital
(e) Net present value, assuming a 14% cost of capital
(f) Profitability index, assuming a 10% cost of capital
(g) Profitability index, assuming a 14% cost of capital

(h) Internal rate of return

(i) Modified internal rate of return, assuming reinvestment at 10%

(j) Modified internal rate of return, assuming reinvestment at 14%

3. You are evaluating an investment project, Project XX, with the following cash flows:

Period	Cash flow
0	−$200,000
1	65,000
2	65,000
3	65,000
4	65,000
5	65,000

Calculate the following:

(a) Payback period

(b) Discounted payback period, assuming a 10% cost of capital

(c) Discounted payback period, assuming a 15% cost of capital

(d) Net present value, assuming a 10% cost of capital

(e) Net present value, assuming a 15% cost of capital

(f) Profitability index, assuming a 10% cost of capital

(g) Profitability index, assuming a 15% cost of capital

(h) Internal rate of return

(i) Modified internal rate of return, assuming reinvestment at 10%

(j) Modified internal rate of return, assuming reinvestment at 15%

4. You are evaluating an investment project, Project WW, with the following cash flows:

Period	End of period cash flow
0	−$100,000
1	0
2	0
3	0
4	174,901

Calculate the following:

(a) Payback period

(b) Discounted payback period, assuming a 10% cost of capital

(c) Discounted payback period, assuming a 12% cost of capital

(d) Net present value, assuming a 10% cost of capital

(e) Net present value, assuming a 12% cost of capital
(f) Profitability index, assuming a 10% cost of capital
(g) Profitability index, assuming a 12% cost of capital
(h) Internal rate of return
(i) Modified internal rate of return, assuming reinvestment at 10%

5. You are evaluating an investment project, Project VV, with the following cash flows:

Period	End-of-period cash flow
0	−$100,000
1	20,000
2	40,000
3	60,000

Calculate the following:
(a) Payback period
(b) Discounted payback period, assuming a 5% cost of capital
(c) Discounted payback period, assuming a 10% cost of capital
(d) Net present value, assuming a 5% cost of capital
(e) Net present value, assuming a 10% cost of capital
(f) Profitability index, assuming a 5% cost of capital
(g) Profitability index, assuming a 10% cost of capital
(h) Internal rate of return

6. Suppose you are evaluating two mutually exclusive projects, Thing 1 and Thing 2, with the following cash flows:

	End-of-year cash flows	
Year	Thing 1	Thing 2
2000	−$10,000	−$10,000
2001	3,293	0
2002	3,293	0
2003	3,293	0
2004	3,293	14,641

(a) If the cost of capital on both projects is 5%, which project, if any, would you choose? Why?
(b) If the cost of capital on both projects is 8%, which project, if any, would you choose? Why?
(c) If the cost of capital on both projects is 11%, which project, if any, would you choose? Why?

(d) If the cost of capital on both projects is 14%, which project, if any, would you choose? Why?

(e) At what discount rate would you be indifferent between choosing Thing 1 and Thing 2?

(f) On the same graph, draw the investment profiles of Thing 1 and Thing 2. Indicate the following items:

- cross-over discount rate
- NPV of Thing 1 if the cost of capital is 5%
- NPV of Thing 2 if cost of capital is 5%
- IRR of Thing 1
- IRR of Thing 2

7. Suppose you are evaluating two mutually exclusive projects, Thing 3 and Thing 4, with the following cash flows:

	End-of-year cash flows	
Year	Thing 3	Thing 4
2000	−$10,000	−$10,000
2001	3,503	0
2002	3,503	0
2003	3,503	0
2004	3,503	19,388

(a) If the cost of capital on both projects is 5%, which project, if any, would you choose? Why?

(b) If the cost of capital on both projects is 10%, which project, if any, would you choose? Why?

(c) If the cost of capital on both projects is 15%, which project, if any, would you choose? Why?

(d) If the cost of capital on both projects is 20%, which project, if any, would you choose? Why?

(e) At what discount rate would you be indifferent between choosing Thing 3 and Thing 4?

(f) On the same graph, draw the investment profiles of Thing 3 and Thing 4. Indicate the following items:

- cross-over discount rate
- NPV of Thing 3 if the cost of capital is 10%
- NPV of Thing 4 if the cost of capital is 10%

- IRR of Thing 3
- IRR of Thing 4

8. Suppose you are evaluating two mutually exclusive projects, Thing 5 and Thing 6, with the following cash flows:

Year	End-of-year cash flows	
	Thing 5	Thing 6
2000	−$10,000	−$10,000
2001	2,000	0
2002	5,000	0
2003	6,000	13,500

(a) If the cost of capital on both projects is 0%, which project, if any, would you choose? Why?

(b) If the cost of capital on both projects is 10%, which project, if any, would you choose? Why?

(c) If the cost of capital on both projects is 15%, which project, if any, would you choose? Why?

(d) If the cost of capital on both projects is 20%, which project, if any, would you choose? Why?

(e) At what discount rate would you be indifferent between choosing Thing 5 and Thing 6?

(f) On the same graph, draw the investment profiles of Thing 5 and Thing 6. Indicate the following items:

- cross-over discount rate
- NPV of Thing 5 if the cost of capital is 15%
- NPV of Thing 6 if the cost of capital is 15%
- IRR of Thing 5
- IRR of Thing 6

9. Consider the results from analyzing the following five projects:

Project	Outlay	NPV
AA	$300,000	$10,000
BB	400,000	20,000
CC	200,000	10,000
DD	100,000	10,000
EE	200,000	−15,000

Suppose there is a limit on the capital budget of $600,000. Which projects should we invest in given our capital budget?

10. Consider these three independent projects:

Period	FF	GG	HH
0	−$100,000	−$200,000	−$300,000
1	30,000	40,000	40,000
2	30,000	40,000	40,000
3	30,000	40,000	40,000
4	40,000	120,000	240,000
Cost of capital	5%	6%	7%

(a) If there is no limit on the capital budget, which projects would you choose? Why?

(b) If there is a limit on the capital budget of $300,000, which projects would you choose? Why?

11. Consider the following four independent projects:

Project	Investment outlay	Net present value
JJ	$100,000	$50,000
KK	$100,000	$60,000
LL	$200,000	$100,000
MM	$200,000	$80,000

If there is a limit of $400,000 for capital projects, which projects should you select? Why?

12. The Mighty Mouse Computer company is considering whether or not to install a packaging robot. The robot costs $500,000, including shipping and installation. The robot can be depreciated using MACRS as a 5-year asset. (MACRS depreciation rates for a five-year asset: 20%, 32%, 19.2%, 11.52%, 11.52%, and 5.76%.) The robot is expected to last for five years, at which time management expects to sell it for parts for $100,000. The robot is expected to replace five employees in the shipping department, saving the company $150,000 each year. Mighty's tax rate is 30%.

(a) What are the net cash flows for each year of the robot's 5-year life?

(b) What is the net present value of the robot investment if the cost of capital is 10%?

(c) What is the net present value of the robot investment if the cost of capital is 5%?

(d) What is the profitability index of this investment if the cost of capital is 5%?

(e) What is the payback period of the robot investment?

(f) What is the discounted payback period of the robot investment if the cost of capital is 5%?

(g) What is the internal rate of return of the robot investment?

(h) What is the modified internal rate of return of the robot investment if the cash flows are reinvested at 5%?

(i) If the cost of capital is 5%, should Mighty Mouse invest in this robot?

13. The Sopchoppy Motorcycle Company is considering an investment of $600,000 in a new motorcycle. They expect to increase sales in each of the next three years by $400,000, while increasing expenses by $200,000 each year. They expect that they can carve out a niche in the marketplace for this new motorcycle for three years, after which they intend to cease production on this motorcycle and sell the manufacturing equipment for $200,000. Assume the equipment is depreciated at the rate of $200,000 each year. Sopchoppy's tax rate is 40%.

(a) What are the net cash flows for each year of the motorcycles 3-year life?

(b) What is the net present value of the investment if the cost of capital is 10%?

(c) What is the net present value of the motorcycle investment if the cost of capital is 5%?

(d) What is the profitability index of this investment if the cost of capital is 5%?

(e) What is the payback period of the investment?

(f) What is the discounted payback period of the investment if the cost of capital is 5%?

(g) What is the internal rate of return of the investment?

(h) What is the modified internal rate of return of the motorcycle investment if the cash flows are reinvested at 5%?

(i) If the cost of capital is 10%, should Sopchoppy invest in this motorcycle?

14. Using the cash flows provided in Chapter 3 for the Williams 5 & 10, calculate the net present value of opening the new retail store if the cost of capital is 10%.

15. Using the cash flows provided in Chapter 3 for the Hirshleifer Company, calculate the net present value of replacement of facilities decision if the cost of capital is 10%.

16. The Leontif Company is evaluating the purchase of a new computer for its marketing department, replacing its existing computer. The current computer is fully depreciated and has little or no resale value. The new computer would cost $40,000 and would be depreciated for tax purposes as a 5-year asset using MACRS. The new computer would not enhance revenues but would reduce expenses due to increased operating efficiency. It is expected that the computer would be used for four years, at which time it would have a resale value of $1,000.

    The Leontif Company's income is taxed at 37%. Leontif requires projects with similar risk to provide a return of 10%. What would the amount of expense reduction have to be in order for this computer to be considered attractive to Leontif? Assume that any expense reduction is the same for each year of operating this new computer.

17. The B. Bowden Company is evaluating the purchase of a stadium, the B. B. Dome. The stadium would cost Bowden $1 million and would be depreciated for tax purposes using straight-line over 20 years (that is, $50,000 per year). It is expected that the stadium will increase B. Bowden revenues by $400,000 per year, but would also increase expenses by $200,000 per year. B. Bowden would be expected to increase its working capital by $20,000 to accommodate the increased investment in ticket accounts receivable. B. Bowden Company intends to sell the stadium to the city after ten years for $600,000. The marginal tax rate for B. Bowden is 40%. For purposes of identifying the timing of cash flows, consider the purchase to be made at the end of 2000, the first year of operations the year 2001, and the last year of operations the year 2010.

(a) Calculate the net cash flows for each year, 2000 through 2010.

(b) If the cost of capital for this project is 10%, should Bowden invest in the new stadium?

(c) Over what range of cost of capital would this project be attractive? Over what range of cost of capital would this project be unattractive?

18. The Rockafeller Music Company is considering expanding its production line to satisfy the demand for more CDs. The company has commissioned consultant studies for the expansion, spending $200,000 for these studies. The results of the studies indicate that the firm must spend $1 million on a new building and $500,000 on production equipment. The consultants' report predicts that the company can increase its revenues by $400,000 each year, while incurring an increase of $160,000 in expenses. The consultants expect rivals to step up production within five years, reducing benefits from the expansion to Rockafeller after five years. Therefore, a 5-year time horizon is assumed for this expansion project. The expansion would require that the company increase it currents assets by $100,000 initially, but these asset accounts will be returned to previous levels at the end of the project.

Assume that the building is depreciated using straight-line over a 20-year period and that it can be sold at the end of five years for $800,000. Further assume that the equipment is depreciated using straight-line over a 10-year period and that it can be sold at the end of five years for $150,000. The marginal tax rate of Rockafeller is 40%. The cost of capital for this project is 10%. Should Rockafeller invest in this project? Explain.

Section III

Capital Budgeting and Risk

All new projects involve risk. Capital budgeting decisions require that managers analyze the following factors for each project they consider:

- Future cash flows
- The degree of uncertainty of these future cash flows
- The value of these future cash flows considering their uncertainty

We described how to estimate future cash flows in Section I where we saw that a project's incremental cash flows comprise two types: (1) operating cash flows (the change in the revenues, expenses, and taxes), and (2) investment cash flows (the acquisition and disposition of the project's assets).

In Section II, we focused on evaluating future cash flows. *Given* estimates of incremental cash flows for a project and *given* a discount rate that reflects the uncertainty that the project will produce those flows as expected, we looked at alternative techniques that are used to select projects to invest in.

In deciding whether a project increases shareholder wealth, managers must weigh its benefits and its costs. The costs are:

1. The cash flow necessary to make the investment (the investment outlay), and
2. The opportunity costs of using the cash tied up in this investment.

The benefits are the future cash flows generated by the investment. But the future is uncertain, therefore future cash flows are uncertain. So, for an evaluation of any investment to be meaningful, we must evaluate the risk that its cash flows will differ from what is expected, in terms of the amount and the timing of the cash flows. *Risk* is the *degree* of uncertainty.

Managers incorporate risk into their calculations in one of two ways: (1) by discounting future cash flows using a higher discount rate, the greater the cash flow's risk, or (2) by requiring a higher annual return on a project, the greater the cash flow's risk. In Section III, we look at the sources of cash flow uncertainty and how to incorporate risk in the capital budgeting decision.

Below we describe what we mean by risk in the context of long-lived projects. In Chapter 10 we propose several commonly used statistical measures of risk applied to capital projects. In Chapter 11, we then look at the relation between risk and return, specifically for capital projects, and we conclude by showing how risk can be incorporated in the capital budgeting decision.

RISK AND CASH FLOWS

When managers estimate what it costs to invest in a given project and what its benefits will be in the future, they are coping with uncertainty. The uncertainty arises from different sources, depending on the type of investment being considered, as well as the circumstances and the industry in which it is operating. Uncertainty may result from:

- *Economic conditions*. Will consumers be spending or saving? Will the economy be in a recession? Will the government stimulate spending? Will there be inflation?
- *Market conditions*. Is the market competitive? How long does it take competitors to enter into the market? Are there any barriers, such as patents or trademarks, that will keep competitors away? Is there a sufficient supply of raw materials and labor? How much will raw materials and labor cost in the future?
- *Taxes*. What will tax rates be? Will Congress alter the tax system?
- *Interest rates*. What will be the cost of raising capital in future years?

- *International conditions.* Will the exchange rate between different countries' currencies change? Are the governments of the countries in which the firm does business stable?

These sources of uncertainty influence future cash flows. To choose projects that will maximize owners' wealth, we need to assess the uncertainty associated with a project's cash flows. In evaluating a capital project, we are concerned with measuring its risk.

The Required Rate of Return

Financial managers worry about risk because the suppliers of capital — the creditors and owners — demand compensation for taking on risk. They can either provide their funds to your firm to make investments or they could invest their funds elsewhere. Therefore, there is an opportunity cost to consider: what the suppliers of capital could earn elsewhere for the same level of risk. We refer to the return required by the suppliers of capital as the *cost of capital*, which comprises the compensation to suppliers of capital for their opportunity cost of not having the funds available (the time value of money) and compensation for risk.

Cost of capital = compensation for the time value money
+ compensation for risk

Using the net present value criterion, if the present value of the future cash flows is greater than the present value of the cost of the project, it is expected to increase the value of the firm and therefore is acceptable. And under certain circumstances, using the internal rate of return criterion, if the project's return exceeds the project's cost of capital, the project increases owners' wealth. From the perspective of the firm, this required rate of return is what it costs to raise capital, so we also refer to this rate as the cost of capital.

We refer to the compensation for risk as a *risk premium* — the additional return necessary to compensate investors for the risk they bear. How much compensation for risk is enough? 2%? 4%? 10%?

How do we assess the risk of a project? We begin by recognizing that the assets of a firm are the result of its prior investment decisions. Therefore, a firm is really a collection or portfolio of projects. So when the firm adds another project to its portfolio, should we be concerned only about the risk of that additional project? Or should we be concerned about the risk of the entire portfolio when the new project is included in it? To answer this question, let's look at the different dimensions of risk of a project.

Stand-Alone versus Market Risk

If we have some idea of the uncertainty associated with a project's future cash flows — its possible outcomes — and the probabilities associated with these outcomes, we will have a measure of the risk of the project. But this is the project's risk in isolation from the firm's other projects, also referred to as the project's *total risk*, or *stand-alone risk*.

Since most firms have many assets, the stand-alone risk of a project under consideration may not be the relevant risk for analyzing the project. A firm is a portfolio of assets, and the returns of these different assets are not perfectly positively correlated with one another. We are therefore not concerned about the stand-alone risk of a project, but rather *how the addition of the project to the firm's portfolio of assets changes the risk of the firm's portfolio.*

Now let's take it a step further. Shareholders own shares of many firms and these shareholders are investors who *themselves* may hold diversified portfolios. These investors are concerned about how the firm's investments affect the risk of their own personal portfolios. When owners demand compensation for risk, they are requiring compensation for market risk, the risk they can't get rid of by diversifying. Recognizing this, a firm considering taking on a new project should be concerned with how it changes its market risk. Therefore, if the firm's owners hold diversified investments, it is the project's *market* risk that is relevant to the firm's decision making.

If the Microsoft Corporation introduces a new operating system, the relevant risk to consider in evaluating this new product is not its stand-alone risk, but rather it market risk. Microsoft has many computer software products and services — they have a portfolio of investments. And while its investments are all related somewhat to computers, the products' fortunes do not rise and fall perfectly in sync with one another — in other words, some of the risk is diversified away. Additionally, investors who hold Microsoft common stock in their portfolios also own stock of other corporations (and perhaps own some bonds, real estate, or cash). What risk is relevant for Microsoft to consider in its decision regarding the new product? The market risk of the product since some risk is diversified away at the company level and some risk is diversified away at the investors' level.

Even though we generally believe that it's the project's market risk that is important to analyze, stand-alone risk should not be ignored. If we are making decisions for a small, closely held firm, whose owners do not hold well-diversified portfolios, the stand-alone risk gives us a good idea of the project's risk. And many small businesses fit into this category.

And even if we are making investment decisions for large corporations that have many products and whose owners are well-diversified, the analysis of stand-alone risk is useful. Stand-alone risk is often closely related to market risk: in many cases, projects with higher stand-alone risk may also have higher market risk. And a project's stand-alone risk is easier to measure than market risk. We can get an idea of a project's stand-alone risk by evaluating the project's future cash flows using statistical measures, sensitivity analysis, and simulation analysis. We now consider these evaluation techniques.

Chapter 10

Measurement of Project Risk

The financial decision-maker needs to measure risk to incorporate it into the capital budgeting decision. We next look at several methods of evaluating risk, focusing first on stand-alone risk and then on market risk.

MEASURING A PROJECT'S STAND-ALONE RISK

We will look at three statistical measures used to evaluate the risk associated with a project's possible outcomes: the range, the standard deviation, and the coefficient of variation. Let's demonstrate each using new products as examples. Based on experience with our firm's current product lines and the market research for new Product A, we can estimate that it may generate one of three different cash flows in its first year, depending on economic conditions:

Economic condition	Cash flow	Probability
Boom	$10,000	20% or 0.20
Normal	5,000	50% or 0.50
Recession	−1,000	30% or 0.30

Statistical Measures of Cash Flow Risk

Looking at this table we can see there is more than one possible outcome. There are three possible outcomes, each representing a possible cash flow and its probability of occurring. Product A's three possible cash flows are represented graphically in Exhibit 1. Looking at this graph, we see that there is some chance of getting a −$1,000 cash flow and some chance of getting a +$10,000 cash flow, though the most likely possibility (the one with the greatest probability) is a +$5,000 cash flow.

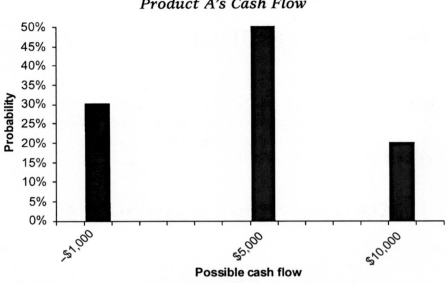

Exhibit 1: Probability Distribution for Product A's Cash Flow

But to get an idea of Product A's risk, we need to know a bit more. The more spread out the possible outcomes, the greater the degree of uncertainty (the risk) of what is expected in the future. We refer to the degree to which future outcomes are "spread out" as *dispersion*. In general, the greater the dispersion, the greater the risk.

There are several measures we could use to describe the dispersion of future outcomes. We will focus on the range, the standard deviation, and the coefficient of variation.

The Range

The *range* is a statistical measure representing how far apart are the two extreme outcomes of the probability distribution. The range is calculated as the difference between the best and the worst possible outcomes:

Range = best possible outcome − worst possible outcome

For Product A, the range of possible outcomes is $10,000 − (−$1,000) = $11,000. The larger the range, the farther apart are the two extreme possible outcomes and therefore more risk.

The Standard Deviation

Though easy to calculate, the range doesn't tell us anything about the likelihood of the possible cash flows at or between the extremes. In financial decision-making, we are interested in not just the extreme outcomes but all the possible outcomes.

One way to characterize the dispersion of all possible future outcomes is to look at how the outcomes differ from one another. This would require looking at the differences between all possible outcomes and trying to summarize these differences in a usable measure.

An alternative to this is to look at how each possible future outcome differs from a single value, comparing each possible outcome with this one value. A common approach is to use a measure of central location of a probability distribution, the *expected value.*

Let's use N to designate the number of possible future outcomes, x_n to indicate the nth possible outcome, p_n to indicate the probability of the nth outcome occurring, and $E(x)$ to indicate the expected outcome. The expected cash flow is the weighted average of the cash flows, where the weights are the probabilities:

$$E(x) = x_1 p_1 + x_2 p_2 + x_3 p_3 + ... + x_n p_n + ... + x_N p_N$$

or, using summation notation,

$$E(x) = \sum_{n=1}^{N} p_n x_n$$

The *standard deviation* is a measure of how each possible outcome deviates — that is, differs — from the expected value. The standard deviation provides information about the dispersion of possible outcomes because it provides information on the distance each outcome is from the expected value and the likelihood the outcome will occur. The standard deviation is:

$$\sigma(x) = \sqrt{\sum_{n=1}^{N} p_n [x_n - E(x)]^2}$$

The calculation of the standard deviation is shown in Exhibit 2. As you can see, it is necessary to calculate the expected value before calculating the standard deviation. The standard deviation of Product A's future cash flows is $3,894.

Exhibit 2: Calculation of the Standard Deviation of the Possible Cash Flows of Product A

Economic conditions	Cash flow	Probability	$x_n p_n$	$x_n - E(x)$	$(x_n - E(x))^2$	$p_n (x_n - E(x))^2$
Boom	$10,000	0.20	$2,000	$5,800	33,640,000	6,728,000
Normal	5,000	0.50	2,500	800	640,000	320,000
Recession	−1,000	0.30	−300	−5,200	27,040,000	9,112,000
		$E(x) =$	$4,200		$\sigma^2(x) =$	15,160,000

Standard deviation = $\sigma(x) = \sqrt{15,160,000}$ = $3,894

The standard deviation is a statistical measure of dispersion of the possible outcomes about the expected outcome. The larger the standard deviation, the greater the dispersion and, hence, the greater the risk.

Let's look at another example. Suppose the possible cash flows and their corresponding probabilities in the first year for Product B are:

Cash Flow	Probability
$10,000	5%
9,000	10
8,000	20
7,000	30
6,000	20
5,000	10
4,000	5

Expected value and standard deviation calculated similar to that of Product A is shown in Exhibit 2. We can describe the probability distribution with several measures:

- the expected value is $7,000;
- the most likely outcome — the one that has the highest probability of occurring — is $7,000;
- range of possible outcomes is $10,000 − 4,000 = $6,000; and
- the standard deviation of the possible outcomes is $1,449.

Let's compare the risk associated with Product B's cash flows with the risk of still another project, Product C, which has the following possible cash flows:

Cash Flow	Probability
$10,000	2%
9,000	8
8,000	20
7,000	40
6,000	20
5,000	8
4,000	2

Describing the possible outcomes for Product C (which you can determine on your own applying what we did for Products A and B),

- the expected value is $7,000;
- the most likely outcome is $7,000;
- the range of possible outcomes is $6,000; and
- the standard deviation of the possible outcome is $1,183.

Both B and C have the same most likely outcome, the same expected value, and the same range of possible outcomes. But the standard deviation the cash flows for C is less than it is for B. This confirms what we see comparing the probability distributions of Product C, as shown in Exhibit 3 — the distribution of possible outcomes of Product C are less disperse than that of Product B.

Exhibit 3: Probability Distributions of Product B and Product C

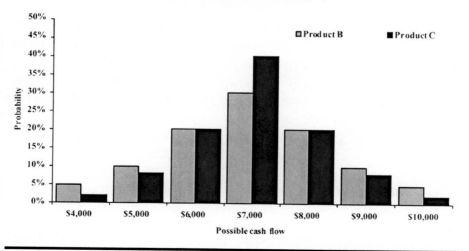

The Coefficient of Variation

The standard deviation provides a useful measure of dispersion. It is a measure of how widely dispersed the possible outcomes are from the expected value. However, we cannot compare standard deviations of different projects' cash flows if they have different expected values. To see this, consider the possible cash flows from Product D:

Cash Flow	Probability
$100,000	5%
90,000	10
80,000	20
70,000	30
60,000	20
50,000	10
40,000	5

We can describe the probability distribution of Product D's possible cash flows:

- the expected value is $70,000;
- the most likely outcome is $70,000;
- range of possible outcomes is $60,000; and
- the standard deviation of the possible outcomes is $14,491.

Is Product D riskier than Product B? Product D's standard deviation is larger, but so is its expected value. Since Product B's and Product D's cash flows are of different sizes, comparing their standard deviations is meaningless without somehow adjusting for the scale of cash flows.

We can do that with the *coefficient of variation*, which translates the standard deviation of different probability distributions (because their scales differ), so that they can be compared.

The coefficient of variation for a probability distribution is the ratio of its standard deviation to its expected value:

$$\text{Coefficient of variation} = \frac{\sigma(x)}{E(x)}$$

Calculating the coefficient of variation for each of the four products' probability distributions in our examples,

Product	Expected value	Range	Standard deviation	Coefficient of variation
A	$4,200	$11,000	$3,894	0.9271
B	7,000	6,000	1,449	0.2070
C	7,000	6,000	1,183	0.1690
D	70,000	6,000	14,491	0.2070

Comparing coefficients of variation among these products, we see that:

- Product A is the riskiest,
- Product C is least risky, and
- Products B and D have identical risk.

Risk can be expressed statistically in terms of measures such as the range, the standard deviation, and the coefficient of variation. Now that we know how to calculate and apply these statistical measures, all we need are the probability distributions of the project's future cash flows, so we can apply these statistical tools to evaluate a project's risk.

Where do we get these probability distributions? From research, judgment, and experience. We can use sensitivity analysis or simulation analysis to get an idea of a project's possible future cash flows and their risk.

Sensitivity Analysis

Estimates of cash flows are based on assumptions about the economy, competitors, consumer tastes and preferences, construction costs, and taxes, among a host of other possible assumptions. One of the first things managers must consider about these estimates is how sensitive they are to these assumptions. For example, if we only sell 2 million units instead of 3 million units in the first year, is the project still profitable? Or, if Congress increases the tax rates, will the project still be attractive?

We can analyze the sensitivity of cash flows to change in the assumptions by reestimating the cash flows for different scenarios. *Sensitivity analysis*, also called *scenario analysis*, is a method of looking at the possible outcomes, given a change in one of the factors in the analysis. Sometimes we refer to this as "what if" analysis — "what if this changes," "what if that changes," and so on.

To see how sensitivity analysis works, let's look at the Williams 5 & 10 cash flows we determined in Chapter 3, where the detailed calculations were shown in Exhibit 1 of that chapter. The net cash flow for each year is:

Year	Net cash flow
Initial	−$550,000
2001	+ 79,809
2002	+ 153,409
2003	+ 149,569
2004	+ 147,265
2005	+ 460,946

Now let's play with the assumptions. Suppose that the tax rate is not known with certainty, but instead the tax rate may be 20%, 30%, or 40%. The tax rate that we assume affects all the following factors:

- The expected tax on the sale of the building and equipment in the last year
- The cash outflow for taxes from the change in revenues and expenses
- The cash inflow from the depreciation tax-shield

Each different tax assumption changes the project's net cash flows as follows:

Year	Tax rate = 20%	Net cash flow Tax rate = 30%	Tax rate = 40%
Initial	−$550,000	−$550,000	−$550,000
2001	+ 86,540	+ 79,909	+ 73,079
2002	+ 168,940	+ 153,409	+ 137,879
2003	+ 166,380	+ 149,569	+ 132,759
2004	+ 164,844	+ 147,265	+ 129,687
2005	+ 467,298	+ 460,946	+489,987

We can see that the value of this project, hence any decision made based on this value, is sensitive to what we assume will be the tax rate.

We could take each of the "what if" tax rate assumptions and re-calculate the value of the investment.

If the tax rate is ...	... the net present value using a cost of capital of 5% is ...
20%	$331,134
30%	276,679
40%	249,954

But when we do this, we have to be careful — the net present value requires discounting the cash flows at a rate that reflects risk

— but *that* is what we are trying to figure out! So we shouldn't be using the net present value method in evaluating a project's risk in our sensitivity analysis.

An alternative is to re-calculate the internal rate of return under each "what if" scenario.

If the tax rate is ...	... the internal rate of return will be ...
20%	20.20%
30%	17.77%
40%	16.32%

And this illustrates one of the attractions of using the internal rate of return to evaluate projects. Despite its drawbacks in the case of mutually exclusive projects and in capital rationing, as pointed out in Chapter 7, the internal rate of return is more suitable to use in assessing a project's attractiveness under different scenarios and, hence, that project's risk. Why? Because the net present value approach requires us to use a cost of capital to arrive at a project's value, but the cost of capital is what we set out to determine! We would be caught in a vicious circle if we used the net present value approach in sensitivity analysis. But the internal rate of return method does not require a cost of capital; instead, we can look at the possible internal rates of return of a project and use this information to measure a project's risk.

If we can specify the probability distribution for tax rates, we can put sensitivity analysis together with the statistical measures of risk. Suppose that in the analysis of the Williams project it is most likely that tax rates be 30%, though there is a slight probability that tax rates will be lowered and a chance that tax rates will be increased. More specifically, suppose the probability distribution of future tax rates and, hence the project's internal rate of return, is:

Probability is ...	that the tax rate will be ...	and hence the internal rate of return will be ...
10%	20%	20.20%
50%	30%	17.77%
40%	40%	16.32%

Applying the calculations for the statistical measures of risk to this distribution,

Expected internal rate of return	=	17.433%
Standard deviation of possible internal rates of return	=	1.148%
Coefficient of variation	=	0.066

We could then judge whether the project's expected return is sufficient considering its risk (as measured by the standard deviation). We could also use these statistical measures to compare this project with other projects under consideration.

Sensitivity analysis illustrates the effects of changes in assumptions. But because sensitivity analysis focuses only on one change at a time, it is not very realistic. We know that not one, but many factors can change throughout the life of a project. In the case of the Williams project, there are a number of assumptions built into the analysis that are based on uncertainty, including the sales prices of the building and equipment in five years and the entrance of competitors no sooner than five years. And you can use your imagination and envision any new product and the attendant uncertainties including the economy, the firm's competitors, and the price and supply of raw material and labor.

Simulation Analysis

Sensitivity analysis becomes unmanageable if we change several factors at the same time. A manageable approach to changing two or more factors at the same time is computer simulation. *Simulation analysis* allows the financial manager to develop a probability distribution of possible outcomes, given a probability distribution for each variable that may change.

Suppose you are analyzing a project having the following uncertain elements:

- Sales (number of units and price)
- Costs
- Tax rate

Suppose further that the initial outlay for the project is known with certainty and so is the rate of depreciation. From the firm's marketing research, you estimate a probability distribution for dollar sales. And from the firm's engineers and production management, and purchasing agents, you estimate the probability distribution for costs, which depends, in part, on the number of units sold. The firm's economists estimate the probability distribution of possible tax rates.

You have three probability distributions to work with. Now you need a computer simulation program to meet your needs — one that can:

- randomly select a possible value of unit sales for each year, given the probability distribution;
- randomly select a possible value of costs for each year, given the unit sales and the probability distribution of costs; and
- randomly select a tax rate for each year, given the probability distribution of tax rates.

While the computer cannot roll a die, spin a wheel like they do in TV game shows, or select ping-pong balls with numbers as they do with lotteries, computers can be programmed to randomly select values based on whatever probability distribution you want. For example, @Risk allows the financial manager to assume probability distributions for different variables in an analysis and perform simulation.

Once the computer selects the number of units sold, the cost per unit, and the tax rate, the cash flows are calculated, as well as its internal rate of return. You now have one internal rate of return. Then you start all over, with the computer repeating this process, calculating an internal rate of return each time. After a large number of trials, you will have a frequency distribution of the return on investments. A *frequency distribution* is a description of the number of times you've arrived at each different return. Using the statistical measures of risk, you can evaluate the risk associated with the return on investments by applying these measures to this frequency distribution.[1]

---

[1] Because the frequency distribution is a *sampling* distribution (that is, its based on a sample of observations instead of a probability distribution), its standard deviation is calculated in a slightly different manner than the standard deviation of possible outcomes. The standard deviation of a frequency distribution is:

$$\text{Standard deviation of frequency distribution} = \sqrt{\frac{\Sigma(x_i - \bar{x})^2 f_i}{N - 1}}$$

where x_i is the value of a particular outcome, $\bar{x}$ is the average of the outcomes, f_i is the number of times the particular outcome is observed (its frequency), and N is the number of trials (e.g., number of times a coin is flipped). The interpretation of this standard deviation is similar to the interpretation of the standard deviation discussed above.

There are two differences between the standard deviation of the frequency distribution and that of the probability distribution: instead of the probability, the weights are the frequency, and the sum of the weighted outcomes is divided by the number of trials (less one).

Simulation analysis is more realistic than sensitivity analysis because it introduces uncertainty for many variables in the analysis. But if you use your imagination, this analysis may become complex since there are interdependencies among many variables in a given year and interdependencies among the variables in different time periods.

However, simulation analysis looks at a project in isolation, focusing instead on a single project's total risk. And simulation analysis also ignores the effects of diversification for the owners' personal portfolio. If owners hold diversified portfolios, then their concern is how a project affects their portfolio's risk, not the project's total risk.

MEASURING A PROJECT'S MARKET RISK

If we are looking at an investment in a share of stock, we could compare the stock's returns and the returns of the entire market over the same period of time as a way of measuring its market risk. While this is not a perfect measurement, it at least provides an estimate of the sensitivity of that particular stock's returns as compared to the returns of the market as a whole. But what if we are evaluating the market risk of a new product? We can't look at how that new product has affected the firm's stock return! So what do we do?

Though we can't look at a project's returns and see how they relate to the returns on the market as a whole, we can do the next best thing: estimate the market risk of the stock of *another firm* whose only line of business is the same as the project's. If we could find such a company, we could look at its stock's market risk and use that as a first step in estimating the project's market risk.

Let's use a measure of market risk, referred to as *beta* and represented by β. β is a measure of the sensitivity of an asset's returns to change in the returns of the market. β is an elasticity measure: if the return on the market increases by 1%, we expect the return on an asset with a β of 2.0 to increase by 2%, if the return on the market decreases by 1%, we expect the returns on an asset with a β of 1.5 to decrease by 1.5%, and so on. The β of an asset, therefore, is a measure of the asset's market risk. To distinguish the beta of an asset from the beta we used for a firm's stock, we refer to an asset's beta as β_{asset} and the beta of a firm's stock as β_{equity}.

Market Risk and Financial Leverage

If a firm has no debt, the market risk of its common stock is the same as the market risk of its assets. This is to say, the beta of its equity, β_{equity}, is the same as the beta of its assets, β_{asset}.

Financial leverage is the use of fixed payment obligations, such as notes or bonds, to finance a firm's assets. The greater the use of debt obligations, the more financial leverage and the greater the risk associated with cash flows to owners. So the effect of using debt is to increase the risk of the firm's equity. If the firm has debt obligations, the market risk of its common stock is *greater* than its assets' risk (that is, $\beta_{equity} > \beta_{asset}$), due to financial leverage. Let's see why.

Consider an asset's beta, β_{asset}. This beta depends on the asset's risk, *not* on how the firm chose to finance it. The firm can choose to finance it with equity only, in which case $\beta_{asset} = \beta_{equity}$. But what if, instead, the firm chooses to finance it partly with debt and partly with equity? When it does this, the creditors and the owners share the risk of the asset, so the asset's risk is split between them, but not equally because of the nature of the claims. Creditors have seniority and receive a fixed amount (interest and principal), so there is less risk associated with a dollar of debt financing than a dollar of equity financing of the same asset. So the market risk borne by the creditors is different than the market risk borne by owners.

Let's represent the market risk of creditors as β_{debt} and the market risk of owners as β_{equity}. Since the asset's risk is shared between creditors and owners, we can represent the asset's market risk as the weighted average of the firm's debt beta, β_{debt}, and equity beta, β_{equity}:[2]

$$\beta_{asset} = \beta_{debt}\left(\frac{debt}{debt + equity}\right) + \beta_{equity}\left(\frac{equity}{debt + equity}\right)$$

But interest on debt is deducted to arrive at taxable income, so the claim that creditors have on the firm's assets does not cost the firm the full amount but rather the after-tax claim. Therefore, the

---

[2] The process of breaking down the firm's beta into equity and debt components is attributed to Robert S. Hamada, "The Effect of the Firm's Capital Structure on the Systematic Risk of Common Stocks," *Journal of Finance* (May 1972): 435–452.

burden of debt financing is actually less due to interest deductibility. Let τ represent the marginal tax rate. The asset beta is:

$$\beta_{\text{asset}} = \beta_{\text{debt}}\left(\frac{(1-\tau)\text{debt}}{(1-\tau)\text{debt} + \text{equity}}\right) + \beta_{\text{equity}}\left(\frac{\text{equity}}{(1-\tau)\text{debt} + \text{equity}}\right)$$

If the firm's debt does not have market risk, $\beta_{\text{debt}} = 0$. This means that the returns on debt do not vary with returns on the market. We generally assumed this to be true for most large firms. Therefore, the market risk of a firm's equity is affected by both the assets' market risk and the nondiversifiable portion of firm's financial risk. If $\beta_{\text{debt}} = 0$,

$$\beta_{\text{asset}} = \beta_{\text{equity}}\left[\frac{\text{equity}}{(1-\tau)\text{debt} + \text{equity}}\right] = \beta_{\text{equity}}\left[\frac{1}{1 + \dfrac{(1-\tau)\text{debt}}{\text{equity}}}\right]$$

This means that an asset's beta is related to the firm's equity beta, with adjustments for financial leverage.[3] You'll notice that if the firm does not use debt, $\beta_{\text{asset}} = \beta_{\text{equity}}$ and if the firm does use debt, $\beta_{\text{asset}} < \beta_{\text{equity}}$.

Therefore, we can translate a β_{equity} into a β_{asset} by removing the firm's financial risk from its β_{equity}. As you can see from the above, to do this we need to know:

- the firm's marginal tax rate
- the amount of the firm's debt financing
- the amount of the firm's equity financing

If the firm's β_{equity}, is 1.2, its marginal tax rate is 40%, and it has \$4 million of debt and \$6 million of equity, its asset risk is 0.8571:

$$\beta_{\text{asset}} = 1.2\left[\frac{1}{1 + \dfrac{(1-0.40)\$4 \text{ million}}{\$6 \text{ million}}}\right] = 1.2(0.7143) = 0.8571$$

---

[3] This means that we can also specify the firm's equity beta in terms of its asset beta:

$$\beta_{\text{equity}} = \beta_{\text{asset}}\left(1 + \frac{(1 - \text{marginal tax rate})\text{debt}}{\text{equity}}\right)$$

The greater a firm's use of debt (relative to equity), the greater its equity's beta and hence the greater its equity's market risk.

Exhibit 4: Equity and Asset Betas for Selected Firms with a Single Line of Business ("Pureplays"), 2000

Company	Line of business	Equity beta	Debt-to-equity ratio	Asset beta
Alcan, Inc.	Aluminum	1.19	0.343	0.973
Clorox	Consumer products	0.57	0.328	0.470
Gap	Retail apparel	1.14	0.194	1.013
McDonalds	Food service	0.67	0.346	0.547

Note: The book value of debt is used in place of the market value of debt since the latter is not readily available. The market value of equity is the product of the number of shares outstanding and the closing share prices as of the end of the year.

The process of translating an equity beta into an asset beta is referred to as *unlevering* since we are removing the effects of financial leverage from the equity beta, β_{equity}, to get a beta for the firm's assets, β_{asset}.[4]

Using a Pure-Play

A firm with a single line of business is referred to as a *pure-play*. Selecting the firm or firms that have a single line of business, where this line of business is similar to the project's, helps in estimating the market risk of a project. We estimate a project's asset beta by starting with the pure-play's equity beta. We can estimate the pure-play's equity beta by looking at the relation between the returns on the pure-play's stock and the returns on the market. Once we have the pure-play's equity beta, we can then "unlever" it by adjusting it for the financial leverage of the pure-play firm.

Examples of pure-play equity betas are shown in Exhibit 4. The firms listed in this table have one primary line of business. Using the information in Exhibit 4 for Alcan Aluminum and assuming a marginal tax rate of 35%, we see that the asset beta for aluminum products is 0.973:

$$\beta_{asset} = 1.19\left[\frac{1}{1+[(1-0.35)0.343]}\right] = 0.973$$

A firm with little debt relative to equity, such as Gap, Inc., will have an asset beta that is close to its equity beta.

---

[4] The effect of financial leverage on equity betas and the process of levering and unlevering betas is attributed to Hamada, "The Effect of the Firm's Capital Structure on the Systematic Risk of Common Stocks."

Since many U.S. corporations whose stock's returns are readily available have more than one line of business, *finding* an appropriate pure-play firm may be difficult. Care must be taken to identify those that have lines of business similar to the project's.

Chapter 11

Incorporating Risk in the Capital Budgeting Decision

I n using the net present value method to value future cash flows, we know that the discount rate should reflect the project's risk. In using the internal rate of return method, we know that the hurdle rate — the minimum rate of return on the project — should reflect the project's risk. Both the net present value and the internal rate of return methods, therefore, depend on using a cost of capital that reflects the project's risk.

RISK-ADJUSTED RATE

The cost of capital is the cost of funds (from creditors and owners). The cost of capital can be viewed as the sum what suppliers of capital demand for providing funds if the project were risk-free plus compensation for the risk they take on.

The compensation for the time value of money includes compensation for any anticipated inflation. We typically use a risk-free rate of interest, such as the yield on a long-term U.S. Treasury bond, to represent the time value of money.

The compensation for risk is the extra return required because the project's future cash flows are uncertain. If we assume that the relevant risk is the stand-alone risk (say, for a small, closely held business), the greater the project's stand-alone risk the greater the return. If we assume that the relevant risk is the project's market risk, the greater the project's market risk the greater the return that investors require.

Return Required for the Project's Market Risk

Now let's explain how to determine the premium for bearing market risk. We do this by first specifying the premium for bearing the average amount of risk for the market as a whole. Then, using our measure of market risk, fine tune this to reflect the market risk of the asset.

The market risk premium for the market as a whole is the difference between the average expected market return, r_m, and the risk-free rate of interest, r_f. If you bought an asset whose market risk was the same as that as the market as a whole, you would expect a return of $r_m - r_f$ to compensate you for market risk.

Next, let's adjust this market risk premium for the market risk of the particular project by multiplying it by that project's asset beta, β_{asset}:

Compensation for market risk = $\beta_{asset} (r_m - r_f)$

This is the extra return necessary to compensate for the project's market risk. The β_{asset} fine tunes the risk premium for the market as a whole to reflect the market risk of the particular project. If we then add the risk-free interest rate, we arrive at the cost of capital:

Cost of capital = $r_f + \beta_{asset} (r_m - r_f)$

Suppose the expected risk-free rate of interest is 4% and the expected return on the market as a whole is 10%. If the β_{asset} is 2.00, this means that if there is a 1% change in the market risk premium, we expect a 2% change in the return on the project. In this case, the cost of capital is 16%:

Cost of capital = 0.04 + 2.00 (0.10 − 0.04) = 0.16, or 16%

If β_{asset} is 0.75, instead, the cost of capital is 8.5%:

Cost of capital = 0.04 + 0.75 (0.06) = 0.085, or 8.5%

If we are able to gauge the market risk of a project, we estimate the risk-free rate and the premium for market risk and put them together. But often we are not able to measure the market risk nor even the risk-free rate. So we need another way to approach the estimation of the project's cost of capital.

Adjusting the Firm's Cost of Capital
Another way to estimate the cost of capital for a project without estimating the risk premium directly is to use the firm's average

cost of capital as a starting point. The average cost of capital is the firm's marginal cost of raising one more dollar of capital — the cost of raising one more dollar in the context of all the firm's projects considered altogether, not just the project being evaluated. We can adjust the average cost of capital of the firm to suit the perceived risk of the project using the following decision rules:

- If a new project being considered is *riskier* than the average project of the firm, the cost of capital of the new project is *greater* than the average cost of capital.
- If the new project is *less risky*, its cost of capital is *less* than the average cost of capital.
- If the project is *as risky* as the average project of the firm, the new project's cost of capital is *equal to* the average cost of capital.

As you can tell, altering the firm's cost of capital to reflect a project's cost of capital requires judgement. How much do we adjust it. If the project is riskier than the typical project do we add 2%? 4%? 10%? There is no prescription here. It depends on the judgement and experience of the decision-maker.

REAL OPTIONS

A significant challenge in capital budgeting is dealing with risk. The traditional methods of evaluating projects are being challenged by an alternative approach that applies option pricing methods to real assets, referred to as *real options valuation* (ROV). The interest in ROV arises from the fact that the traditional methods do not consider directly the options available in many investment projects. Though the importance of options in investment opportunities has long been recognized, it is only recently that a great deal of attention has been paid to incorporate options in a meaningful way.[1]

---

[1] For example, Stewart Myers recognized the importance of considering investment opportunities as growth options ["Determinants of Corporate Borrowings," *Journal of Financial Economics* (Spring 1977): 147–176].

Consider the typical options inherent in an investment opportunity: (1) most every project has an option to abandon, though there may be constraints (e.g., legally binding contracts) that affect when this option can be exercised, (2) many projects have the option to expand, and (3) many projects have an option to defer investment, putting off the major investment outlays to some future date.

So how do we consider these options within the context of the traditional methods? One approach is to use sensitivity analysis or simulation analysis. And while these analyses allow a look at the possible outcomes of a decision, they do not provide guidance regarding which course of action — of the many — to take. Another approach is the use of a decision tree analysis, associating probabilities to each of the possible outcomes for an event and mapping out the possible outcomes and the value of the investment opportunity associated with these different outcomes. And while this approach is workable when there are few options associated with a project, option pricing provides a method of analysis that is more comprehensive.

The basic idea of ROV is to consider that the value of a project extends beyond its value as measured by the net present value; in other words, the value of project is supplemented by the value of the options. Because the options are considered strategic decisions, the revised or supplemented net present value is often referred to as the *strategic NPV.* Consider an investment opportunity that has one option associated with it. The strategic NPV is the sum of the traditional NPV (the static NPV) and the value of the option:

Strategic NPV = Static NPV + value of the option

Options on Real Assets

The valuation of stock options is rather complex, but with the assistance of some well-accepted models, such as the Black-Scholes model, we can estimate the value of an option. For example, in the Black-Scholes option pricing formula there are five factors that are important in the valuation of an option:[2]

---

[2] Fischer Black and Myron Scholes, "The Pricing of Options and Corporate Liabilities," *Journal of Political Economy* (May/June 1973): 637–659.

1. The value of the underlying asset, P
2. The exercise price or strike price of the option, E
3. The risk free rate of interest, r
4. The volatility of the value of the underlying asset, σ
5. The time remaining to the expiration of the option, T

Our focus here is to map these factors onto a real asset option. Like other options, real options can be a call option (the option to buy an asset), a put option (the option to sell an asset), or a compound option (an option on an option). And, like other options, real options may be a European option (an option that can only be exercised on the expiration date) or an American option (an option that can be exercised at any time on or before the expiration date).

In general terms, the relation between the factors that affect the value of a stock option and those that affect a real option correspond as follows:

Parameter	Option on a stock	Option on a real asset
P	The stock's price	The present value of cash flows from the investment opportunity (e.g., cash-out price)
E	The strike price of the option	The present value of the delayed capital expenditure or future cost savings
r	The risk-free rate of interest	The risk-free rate of interest
σ	Volatility of stock's price	Uncertainty of the project's cash flows
T	The time to expiration	Project's useful life

Of course, the factors that correspond to a specific options can be better described when we examine the particular option. Consider the option to abandon. In this case, the underlying asset is continuing operations, and so the value of the underlying asset is the present value of the cash flows associated with the asset. The *strike price* or *exercise price* for this option is the exit value or salvage value of the asset. A number of common real options are described in Exhibit 1.

Identifying the options associated with an investment opportunity is the first step. The second step is to value these options. Consider an investment opportunity to defer an investment. This investment opportunity is similar to what a firm experiences in their investment in research and development: an expenditure or series of expenditures are made in research and development, and then sometime in the future, depending on the results of the research and development, the actions of competitors, and the approval of regulators, the firm can then decide whether to go ahead with the investment opportunity.

Real Options: An Example

Let's put some numbers to the analysis of this project. Suppose that research and development for each of the first four years is $2.5 million. And suppose that at the end of the fifth year the firm has an option to either go ahead with the product or simply abandon it. If the firm goes ahead with development of the product, this will require an investment of $80 million at the end of the fifth year. To make the analysis simpler, let's assume that we can sell the investment in the product — that is, cash out — at the end of the fifth year for $100 million.[3]

Using net present value analysis and a discount rate of 20% (continuously compounded), the present value of this investment opportunity is −$1.36 million:[4]

Exhibit 1: Examples of Real Options

Option	Type	Value of underlying asset	Exercise price
To abandon	American put	The present value of the cash flows from the abandoned assets	The exit or salvage value
To defer an investment	American call	The present value of completed project's net operating cash flows	The deferred investment outlay
To abandon during construction	Compound option	The present value of the completed project's cash flows	The investment outlay necessary for the next stage
To contract the scale of a project	European put	The present value of potential cost savings	The costs of re-scaling the project
To expand	European call	The present value of incremental net operating cash flows	The additional investment outlay
To switch inputs or outputs	American put	The present value of the incremental cash flows from the best alternative use	The cost of retooling production or distribution

[3] If this were not a cash-out scenario, the value that would be used here would be the present value of future cash flows.

[4] In the previous chapters, we discounted cash flows at a rate that reflected annual compounding. To be consistent with the valuation of the Black-Scholes option pricing model, continuous compounding is used throughout this example.

in millions	Year					
	0	1	2	3	4	5
Investment	($2.50)	($2.50)	($2.50)	($2.50)	($2.50)	($80.00)
Terminal value	$0.00	$0.00	$0.00	$0.00	$0.00	$100.00
Net cash flow	($2.50)	($2.50)	($2.50)	($2.50)	($2.50)	$20.00
PV investment	($2.50)	($2.05)	($1.68)	($1.37)	($1.12)	($29.43)
PV terminal value	$0.00	$0.00	$0.00	$0.00	$0.00	$36.79
PV of net cash flow	($2.50)	($2.05)	($1.68)	($1.37)	($1.12)	$7.36
Net present value	($1.36)					

Using the traditional capital budgeting, this suggests that we should reject the project because its net present value is less than $0. But wait — we have not considered the valuable option of the deferred investment — the firm can wait until the end of the fifth year to decide whether it wants to commit the additional $80 million — meanwhile, it invests in the research and development in each of the first four years.

So how much is this option worth? We need to make a couple of assumptions regarding the risk-free rate of interest and volatility. Suppose that the risk free rate of interest is 5%, the market risk premium is 6%, and the volatility (i.e., the standard deviation of the project's cash flows) is 2.5 times that of the market of 20%, or 50%. The cost of capital is calculated using the risk-free rate and the market risk premium is 20%:

$$\text{cost of capital} = 5\% + 6\% \, (50\%/20\%) = 5\% + 15\% = 20\%$$

The value of the factors that are considered in the option valuation are as follows:

Parameter	Value
Value of underlying asset	$36.79 million
Exercise price	$80 million
Risk-free rate of interest	5%
Volatility	50%
Number of periods to exercise	5 years

The value of the underlying asset is the present value of the additional outlays needed to go ahead with the project, discounted at a continuously compounded rate of 20%:

$$\text{Value of underlying asset} = \$100 \text{ million } e^{-0.20 \, (5)} = \$36.79 \text{ million}$$

Using the Black-Scholes option pricing formula, the value of this option is $10.24 million. Does this change the decision of whether to invest? The strategic NPV is

Strategic NPV = Static NPV   + value of the option
Strategic NPV = −$1.36 million + $10.24 million
Strategic NPV = $8.88 million

Hence the project has a positive NPV considering the valuable option that is associated with it.

Challenges

We have simplified this last example to illustrate the importance of considering options. Now let's examine a couple of the challenges in incorporating real option valuation into an actual investment opportunity analysis.

The first challenge has to do with the parameters in the model. Focusing just on the estimate of volatility, we can see that the value added of the option is sensitive to the estimate of volatility. Though we simply assumed that the volatility is 50%, it is not a simple matter to determine the volatility of a project's future cash flow. We experience the same problems that we did in trying to determine the beta of a project — it just isn't measurable directly. The volatility of an investment opportunity's cash flows affect two key elements of the strategic value: the volatility has a positive relation to the value of the option (that is, the greater the volatility, the greater the value of the option), and the volatility has a negative relation to the static NPV (that is, the greater the volatility, the greater the cost of capital and hence the lower the static NPV). If we take this last example and calculate the strategic NPV with volatility of 60% and 40%, as well, we see that the value of the option is affected by the choice of volatility:

	Volatility		
	50%	60%	40%
Static NPV	($1.36)	($1.98)	($0.61)
Value of the option	10.24	13.47	6.97
Strategic NPV	$8.88	$11.49	$6.36

Second, most investment projects have several options, some of which interact. For example, if a firm is investing in R&D over a period of years in the development of a new product, there exists at least two options: the option to abandon during development and the option to defer investment. The valuation problem in the case of multiple options is not simply carried out by adding the separate values because the value of one option may affect the value of other options. Solving for the value of options in the case of multiple, interacting options is beyond the Black and Scholes and is quite difficult, requiring the application of numerical methods.[5]

CERTAINTY EQUIVALENTS

An alternative to adjusting the discount rate to reflect risk is to adjust the cash flow to reflect risk. We do this by converting each cash flow and its risk into it's certainty equivalent. A certainty equivalent is the certain cash flow that is considered to be equivalent to the risky cash flow. For example, if the risky cash flow two periods into the future is $1.5 million, the certainty equivalent is the dollar amount of a certain cash flow (that is, a sure thing) that the firm considers to be worth the same. This certainty equivalent could be $1 million, $0.8 million, $1.4 million, or any other amount — which depends on both the degree of riskiness of the $1.5 million risky cash flow and the judgment of the decision-maker.

The certainty equivalent approach of incorporating risk into the net present value analysis is useful for several reasons.

- *It separates the time value of money and risk.* Risk is accounted for in the adjusted cash flows while the time value of money is accounted for in the discount rate.
- *It allows each period's cash flows to be adjusted separately for risk.* This is accomplished by converting each period's cash flows into a certainty equivalent for that time period. The certainty equivalent factor may be different for each period.
- *The decision maker can incorporate preferences for risk.* This is done in determining the certainty equivalent cash flows.

[5] For a discussion of these issues and an example of option interaction, see Lenos Trigeogis, "A Log-Transformed Binomial Numerical Analysis Method for Valuing Complex Multi-Option Investments," *Journal of Financial and Quantitative Analysis* (September 1991): 309–326.

However, there are some disadvantages to using the certainty equiv-alent approach that stymie its application in practice:

- *The net present value of the certainty equivalent is not easily interpreted.* We no longer have the clearer interpretation of the net present value as the increment in shareholder wealth.
- *There is no reliable way of determining the certainty equiva-lent value for each period's cash flow.*

While the certainty equivalents approach sounds great in principle, it sure is tough to apply in practice.

ASSESSMENT OF PROJECT RISK IN PRACTICE

Most U.S. firms consider risk in some manner in evaluating invest-ment projects. But considering risk is usually a subjective analysis as opposed to the more objective results obtainable with simulation or sensitivity analysis.

Firms that use discounted cash flow techniques, such as internal rate of return and net present value methods, tend to use a single cost of capital. But using a single cost of capital for all projects can be hazardous.

Suppose you use the same cost of capital for all your projects. If all of them have the same risk and the cost of capital you are using is appropriate for this level of risk, no problem. But what if you use the same cost of capital but your projects each have *dif-ferent* levels of risk?

Suppose you use a cost of capital that is the cost of capital for the firm's average risk project. What happens when you apply discounted cash flow techniques, such as the net present value or the internal rate of return, and use this one rate? You will end up:

- rejecting profitable projects (which would have increased owners' wealth) that have risk below the risk of the average risk project because you discounted their future cash flows too much, and

• accepting unprofitable projects whose risk is above the risk of the average project, because you did not discount their future cash flows enough.

Firms that use a risk-adjusted discount rate usually do so by classifying projects into risk classes by the type of project. For example, a firm with a cost of capital of 10% may develop from experience the following classes and discount rates:

Type of project	Cost of capital
New product	14%
New market	12%
Expansion	10%
Replacement	8%

Given this set of costs of capital, the financial manager need only figure out what class a project belongs to and then apply the rate assigned to that class.

Firms may also make adjustments in the cost of capital for factors other than the type of project. For example, firms investing in projects in foreign countries will sometimes make an adjustment for the additional risk of the foreign project, such as exchange rate risk, inflation risk, and political risk.

The cost of capital is generally based on an assessment of the firm's overall cost of capital. The firm first evaluates the cost of each source of capital — debt, preferred stock, and common equity. Then each cost is weighted by the proportion of each source to be raised. This average is referred to as the *weighted average cost of capital* (*WACC*).

There are tools available to assist the decision-maker in measuring and evaluating project risk. But much of what is actually done in practice is subjective. Judgment, with a large dose of experience is used more often than scientific means of incorporating risk. Is this bad? Well, the scientific approaches to measurement and evaluation of risk depend, in part, on subjective assessments of risk, the probability distributions of future cash flows and judgements about market risk. So it is possible that by-passing the more technical analyses in favor of completely subjective assessment of risk may result in cost of capital estimates that better reflect the project's risk. But, then again, it may not. The proof may be in the pudding, but it is difficult to assess the "proof" since we cannot tell how well firms could have done had they used more technical analyses.

Questions for Section III

1. Are the required rate of return and the cost of capital the same thing? Explain.

2. Suppose a discount retail chain in considering opening a new outlet in another city. What should they consider in assessing the risk associated with the future cash flows of this new outlet?

3. Suppose a cereal manufacturer is considering a new cereal based on a new, yet-to-be-released feature film. What should the cereal manufacturer consider in assessing the risk associated with the future cash flows from this new cereal?

4. What distinguishes the standard deviation from the coefficient of variation.

5. Suppose you perform calculations and determine that the expected value of first year cash flows is $1,200 and the standard deviation is $500. What does this mean?

6. Outline a procedure you would use to determine the risk of a project.

7. What distinguishes sensitivity analysis from simulation analysis?

8. Suppose you are responsible for determining the cost of capital of a project. How should your approach differ if the firm is a small, one-owner firm, as compared to a large, publicly held corporation?

9. Suppose the Shell Point Company evaluates most projects using the net present value method and a single discount rate that reflects its marginal cost of raising new capital. Can you see any problem with the method used by this company?

10. Suppose a firm is planning to develop a new toy product over the next two years. If the development and market testing is successful, the firm will begin production of the product in two

years, with a goal of reaching the market in two-and-one-half years. What types of options are inherent in this investment opportunity? Are there any options whose values may interact?

11. Suppose the Destin Sand Company's management evaluates investment opportunities by grouping projects into three risk classes: low, average, and high risk. They assign a cost of capital to each group and use this cost of capital to discount a project's future cash flows: 5% for low risk, 10% for average risk, and 15% for high risk projects. Critique the method of adjusting for risk used by this company.

Problems for Section III

1. Consider the probability distribution of the first year cash flows for the ABC Project:

Possible cash flow	Probability
$1,000	20%
$2,000	60%
$3,000	20%

   (a) Calculate the range of possible cash flows
   (b) Calculate the expected cash flow
   (c) Calculate the standard deviation of the possible cash flows
   (d) Calculate the coefficient of variation of the possible cash flows

2. Consider the probability distribution of the first year cash flows for the DEF Project:

Possible cash flow	Probability
$1,000	10%
$2,000	60%
$3,000	30%

   (a) Calculate the range of possible cash flows
   (b) Calculate the expected cash flow
   (c) Calculate the standard deviation of the possible cash flows
   (d) Calculate the coefficient of variation of the possible cash flows.

3. Consider the probability distributions of the first year cash flows of two projects, GHI and JKL:

GHI	JKL
Possible cash flow	Probability
−$5,000	30%
$0	30%
+$7,000	40%

   (a) Calculate the range of possible cash flows for each project
   (b) Calculate the expected cash flow for each project
   (c) Calculate the standard deviation of the possible cash flows for each project
   (d) Calculate the coefficient of variation of the possible cash flows for each project

(e) Which project has more risk? Why?

4. Consider the probability distributions of the first year cash flows of two projects, MNO and PQR:

MNO Possible cash flow	PQR Probability
−$10,000	20%
$0	60%
+$20,000	20%

(a) Calculate the range of possible cash flows for each project
(b) Calculate the expected cash flow for each project
(c) Calculate the standard deviation of the possible cash flows for each project
(d) Calculate the coefficient of variation of the possible cash flows for each project
(e) Which project has more risk? Why?

5. The Avalanche Snow Company is evaluating the purchase of a new snow-making machine. The marketing and production managers have provided the following change in revenues and expenses associated with the new machine, and the accountant has calculated the depreciation on the machine for the next four years. Assume that there are no changes in working capital in each year.

Year	Sales	Expenses	Depreciation
2001	$100,000	$50,000	$25,000
2002	150,000	75,000	25,000
2003	125,000	75,000	25,000
2004	100,000	75,000	25,000

(a) What is the operating cash flow for each year if the tax rate is 30%?
(b) What is the operating cash flow for each year if the tax rate is 40%?
(c) What is the operating cash flow for each year if the tax rate is 50%?
(d) Suppose the probability of a 30% tax rate is 10%, the probability of a 40% tax rate is 30%, and the probability of a 50% tax rate is 60%. What is the expected operating cash flow for Avalanche? What is the standard deviation of operating cash flows?

6. The Sopchoppy Motorcycle Company is considering an investment of $600,000 in a new motorcycle. The company expects to increase sales in each of the next three years by $400,000, while increasing expenses by $200,000 each year. The company expects that it can carve out a niche in the marketplace for this new motorcycle for three years, after which the company intends to cease production on this motorcycle. Assume the equipment is depreciated at the rate of $200,000 each year. Sopchoppy's tax rate is 40%.

   (a) What is the internal rate of return of this project if the company sells the manufacturing equipment for $200,000 at the end of three years?

   (b) What is the internal rate of return of this project if the company sells the manufacturing equipment for $100,000 at the end of three years?

   (c) What is the internal rate of return of this project if the company sells the manufacturing equipment for $300,000 at the end of three years?

   (d) Suppose the following distribution of possible sales prices on the equipment is developed:

Sales price	Probability
$100,000	25%
$200,000	50%
$300,000	25%

   What is the expected internal rate of return for Sopchoppy? What is the standard deviation of these possible internal rates of return?

7. Consider the probability distribution of possible cash flow outcomes for Project XYZ:

Possible cash flow	Probability
$2,000	$\frac{1}{6}$
$4,000	$\frac{2}{3}$
$6,000	$\frac{1}{6}$

   Construct a simulation of the future cash flows using a six-sided die.

   (a) Rolling the die 30 times, what is the distribution of the possible cash flows?

   (b) Rolling the die a total of 60 times, what is the distribution of the possible cash flows?

(c) Draw a frequency distribution of the results of rolling the die 60 times, plotting the frequency of occurrence on the vertical axis and the possible outcomes on the horizontal axis. How does this frequency distribution compare with the probability distribution?

8. Calculate the cost of capital for each of the possible combinations of the compensation for the time value of money and the compensation for risk:

	Time value of money	Compensation for risk
(a)	2%	5%
(b)	4%	6%
(c)	5%	5%
(d)	4%	6%

9. Suppose the compensation for risk is based on the market risk and that market risk is estimated as the product of the asset's beta and the market risk premium for the market as a whole (that is, $r_m - r_f$). Calculate the cost of capital for each of the possible combinations of compensation for the time value of money and compensation for risk:

	Risk-free rate of interest	Asset beta	Market risk premium
(a)	3%	1.00	4%
(b)	4%	0.50	5%
(c)	5%	1.50	6%
(d)	4%	1.00	4%
(e)	5%	1.25	4%

10. Consider the following information based on firms that are in a single line of business:

Company name	Equity beta	Debt in millions	Equity in millions
A	1.6	$320	$461
B.	0.8	$365	$5,186
C	1.3	$1,447	$3,811
D	0.7	$2,332	$1,456
E	1.1	$334	$314

Assuming a marginal tax rate of 34%, calculate the asset beta for each firm.

Section IV

Analyzing the Lease versus Borrow-to-Buy Problem

A *lease* is an agreement giving to another party the right to use an asset for a specified period, in exchange for a periodic payment referred to as the *rent* or *lease payment*. The party who owns the asset is the lessor; the party granted the right to use it is the *lessee*.

Leasing an asset is often an alternative to purchasing it. But there is a difference between leasing and buying: a firm buying an asset can finance it using debt, equity, or some mix of both. A firm leasing that same asset is essentially financing it with debt. This difference affects how we analyze a decision to buy or to lease.

Several models have been proposed in the finance literature, as well as in promotional material circulated by lessors, as to how to evaluate whether an asset should be purchased or leased. The model presented in Chapter 12 in this section is the one suggested by Stewart Myers.[1] The model is appropriate when the firm is in a taxpaying position and can realize in each year the entire tax shield associated with the expenses for a lease or borrow-to-buy decision. In Chapter 14, the model is extended to instances where the firm is currently in a nontaxpaying position but expects to resume paying taxes at some specified future date.[2] These models are appropriate for valuing a *true lease*.[3]

---

[1] The model was developed in Stewart C. Myers, "An Exact Solution to the Lease versus Borrow Problem" (Working paper, London Graduate School of Business Studies, 1975). An application of the model is presented in Stewart C. Myers, David A. Dill, and Alberto J. Bautista, "Valuation of Financial Lease Contracts," *Journal of Finance* (June 1976): 799–819. For a further discussion of the model and of alternative models that can be used, see Richard Brealey and Stewart C. Myers, *Principles of Corporate Finance* (New York: McGraw-Hill, 1981), Chapter 24.

[2] See Julian R. Franks and Stewart D. Hodges, "Valuation of Financial Lease Contracts: A Note," *Journal of Finance* (May 1978): 657–69. The authors also provide a simplified pedagogical derivation of the lease valuation model derived by Myers.

The key concept in the lease versus borrow-to-buy decision is the need to neutralize the financial risk between the two alternative financing methods. The steps in the lease versus borrow-to-buy decision are as follows:

Step 1. Evaluate the acquisition of an asset under normal financing. That is, the usual capital budgeting procedure for evaluating whether an asset is profitable to acquire should be performed.

Step 2. If it is profitable to acquire the services of the asset, then determine the economic value of all the lease proposals that may be available to the firm. At least one economically attractive lease arrangement will justify the acquisition of the asset's service by leasing.

Step 3. If, in the first step, the acquisition of the asset was not economically justified but an attractive lease arrangement is available, then the entire package should be evaluated to determine whether the services of the asset should be acquired. An attractive lease arrangement in and of itself, however, does not warrant the leasing of an asset.

In the three steps discussed above, reference was made to the "economic attractiveness" or "profitability" of an asset. As explained in Section II, there are several techniques that can be employed to evaluate the economic attractiveness of an investment proposal. The technique employed in this chapter is the *net present value* technique. The same technique will also be used to value a leasing arrangement.

It should be pointed out that some assets whose acquisition a firm is considering may not require Step 1. Management may have decided that the services of the asset must be acquired using some other criterion. For example, management may recognize that cer-

---

[3] The true lease offers all of the primary benefits commonly attributed to leasing. Substantial cost savings can often be achieved through the use of tax-oriented true leases in which the lessor claims and retains the tax benefits of ownership and passes through to the lessee most of such tax benefits in the form of reduced lease payments. The lessor claims tax benefits resulting from equipment ownership such as MACRS depreciation deductions, and the lessee deducts the full lease payment as an expense. The lessor in a true lease owns the leased equipment at the end of the lease term.

tain assets, such as a telephone system or a computer, must be available for operations, or a governmental agency may mandate that a firm acquire the services of an asset. In such cases the only issue is whether leasing or borrowing to purchase is the more economically attractive alternative.

Chapter 12

Valuing a Lease

I nvestment proposals with a positive NPV are attractive and may be made even more attractive by an economically beneficial leasing arrangement. An unattractive investment proposal (that is, a proposal with negative NPV) may be turned into an attractive investment proposal if the combined NPV under normal financing (that is, the usual NPV capital budgeting analysis) and the NPV of the leasing arrangement is greater than zero.

For example, suppose you are considering a machine that you believe may be economically beneficial for your firm to acquire. The financial analyst of your firm performs the NPV analysis assuming normal financing and ascertains the NPV to be −$10,000. The financial analyst will recommend that the firm not acquire the machine based on her analysis. Suppose that upon being told that your firm is not interested in purchasing the machine, the manufacturer offers to lease it for most of the machine's expected life. Your financial analyst then evaluates the lease, using the lease valuation model presented below, and determines it to have an NPV in excess of $10,000. Acquiring the economic benefits expected to be provided by the machine using the manufacturer's leasing arrangement would then be economically attractive because the combined NPV (NPV assuming normal financing and NPV of the lease) produces a positive NPV.[1]

---

[1] The decision rule presented in this chapter is absolute; that is, if the value of a lease is positive, it is more economically attractive than borrowing to purchase. The reverse is true if the value of a lease is negative. In practice, however, a small positive or negative value may mean that the firm will be indifferent to the two financing methods. Management must decide what the minimum absolute value of a lease must be so that a clear-cut choice can be made. For example, suppose equipment with a purchase price of $25 million is found to have an NPV of $8 million. Management can lease rather than purchase the equipment. Suppose the value of the lease using the methodology to be explained in this chapter is −$1,000. Although leasing is not economically attractive because the value of the lease is negative, the magnitude of the lease value is small. Management may in this case be indifferent with respect to the two financing alternatives. Moreover, noneconomic factors must be considered.

Several economic models for valuing a lease have been proposed in the literature. The model used here requires the determination of the net present value of the direct cash flow resulting from leasing rather than borrowing to purchase an asset, where the direct cash flow from leasing is discounted using an "adjusted discount rate."[2] The model is derived from "the objective of maximizing the equilibrium market value of the firm, with careful consideration of interactions between the decision to lease and the use of other financing instruments by the lessee."[3]

DIRECT CASH FLOW FROM LEASING

When a firm elects to lease an asset rather than borrow money to purchase the same asset, this decision will have an impact on the firm's cash flow. The cash flow consequences, which are stated relative to the purchase of the asset, can be summarized as follows:

1. There will be a cash inflow equivalent to the cost of the asset.
2. The lessee may or may not forgo some tax credit. For example, prior to the elimination of the investment tax credit, the lessor could pass through to the lessee this credit.
3. The lessee must make periodic lease payments over the life of the lease. These payments need not be the same in each

---

[2] The adjusted discount rate technique presented in this chapter is fundamentally equivalent to and results in the same answer as is obtained by comparing financing provided by a loan that gives the same cash flow as the lease in every future period. This will be illustrated below.

Although the adjusted discount rate technique is fundamentally equivalent to calculating the adjusted present value of a lease, it is less accurate. The adjusted present value technique takes into consideration the present value of the side effects of accepting a project financed with a lease. (The adjusted present value technique was first developed by Stewart C. Myers, "Interactions of Corporate Financing and Investment Decisions: Implications for Capital Budgeting," *Journal of Finance* (March 1974): 1–26. The reason for a possible discrepancy between the solutions to the lease versus borrow-to-buy decision using the adjusted discount rate technique and adjusted present value technique is that different discount rates are applied where necessary in discounting the cash flow when the latter technique is used. (For an explanation of the adjusted present value technique, see Brealey and Myers, *Principles of Corporate Finance* (New York: McGraw-Hill, 1981), Chapter 19. The application to leasing is given in Chapter 24, pp. 534–36.)

[3] Stewart C. Myers, David A. Dill, and Alberto J. Bautista, "Valuation of Financial Lease Contracts," *Journal of Finance* (June 1976): 799.

period. The lease payments are fully deductible for tax purposes if the lease is a true lease. The tax shield is equal to the lease payment times the lessee's marginal tax rate.
4. The lessee forgoes the tax shield provided by the depreciation allowance since it does not own the asset. The tax shield resulting from depreciation is the product of the lessee's marginal tax rate times the depreciation allowance.
5. There will be a cash outlay representing the lost after-tax proceeds from the residual value of the asset.

For example, consider the capital budgeting problem faced by the Hieber Machine Shop Company. The company is considering the acquisition of a machine that requires an initial net cash outlay of $59,400 and will generate a future cash flow for the next five years of $16,962, $19,774, $20,663, $21,895, and $26,825. Assuming a discount rate of 14%, the NPV for this machine was found to be $11,540.

Let's assume that the following information was used to determine the initial net cash outlay and the cash flow for the machine:

Cost of the machine = $66,000
Tax credit[4] = $6,600
Estimated pre-tax residual = $6,000 value after disposal costs
Estimated after-tax proceeds from residual value = $3,600
Economic life of the machine = 5 years

Depreciation is assumed to be as follows:[5]

Year	Depreciation deductions
1	$9,405
2	13,794
3	13,167
4	13,167
5	13,167

---

[4] We use a tax credit in this illustration to show how the model can be applied should Congress decide to introduce some form of tax credit in future tax legislation. In the past, when an investment tax credit has been made available, the depreciable basis of the asset is reduced by one-half of the amount of the tax credit.

Exhibit 1: Worksheet for Direct Cash Flow from Leasing: Hieber Machine Shop Company *

	End of year					
	0	1	2	3	4	5
Cost of machine	$66,000					
Lost tax credit	(6,600)					
Lease payment	(13,500)	($13,500)	($13,500)	($13,500)	($13,500)	
Tax shield from lease payment**	5,400	5,400	5,400	5,400	5,400	
Lost depreciation tax shields***		(3,762)	(5,518)	(5,267)	(5,267)	($5,267)
Lost residual value						(3,600)
Total	$51,300	($11,862)	($13,618)	($13,367)	($13,367)	($8,867)

* Parentheses denote cash outflow.
** Lease payment multiplied by the marginal tax rate (40%).
*** Depreciation for year multiplied by the marginal tax rate (40%).

The same machine may be leased by the Hieber Machine Shop Company. The lease would require five annual payments of $13,500, with the first payment due immediately. The lessor would retain the assumed tax credit. The tax shield resulting from the lease payments would be realized at the time that Hieber Machine Shop Company made the payment. No additional annual expenses will be incurred by Hieber Machine Shop Company by owning rather than leasing (that is, the lease is a net lease). The lessor will not require Hieber Machine Shop Company to guarantee a minimum residual value.

Exhibit 1 presents the worksheet for the computation of the direct cash flow from leasing rather than borrowing to purchase. The marginal tax rate of Hieber Machine Shop Company is assumed to be 40%. The direct cash flow is summarized below:

Year					
0	1	2	3	4	5
$51,300	($11,862)	($13,618)	($13,367)	($13,367)	($8,867)

The direct cash flow from leasing was constructed assuming that (1) the lease is a net lease and (2) the tax benefit associated with an expense is realized in the tax year the expense is incurred. These two assumptions require further discussion.

[5] The depreciation schedule used in this illustration is not consistent with the tax law at the time of this writing and is used for illustrative purposes only. The depreciation in this example is based on a depreciable basis comprised of the cost of the asset, less one-half of the tax credit, or $66,000 − 3,300 = $62,700. The rates of depreciation for the five years, in order, are 15%, 22%, 21%, 21%, and 21%.

First, if the lease is a gross lease instead of a net lease, the lease payments must be reduced by the cost of maintenance, insurance, and property taxes. These costs are assumed to be the same regardless of whether the asset is leased or purchased with borrowed funds. Where have these costs been incorporated into the analysis? The cash flow from owning an asset is constructed by subtracting the additional operating expenses from the additional revenue. Maintenance, insurance, and property taxes are included in the additional operating expenses. There may be instances when the cost of maintenance differs depending on the financing alternative selected. In such cases, an adjustment to the value of the lease must be made.

Second, many firms considering leasing may be currently in a nontaxpaying position but anticipate being in a taxpaying position in the future. The derivation of the lease valuation model presented in the next section does not consider this situation. It assumes that the tax shield associated with an expense can be fully absorbed by the firm in the tax year in which the expense arises. There is a lease valuation model that will handle under certain conditions the situation of a firm currently in a nontaxpaying position. The generalized model is explained and illustrated in Chapter 14.

VALUING THE DIRECT CASH FLOW FROM LEASING

Because the lease displaces debt, the direct cash flow from leasing should be further modified by devising a loan that in each period except the initial period engenders a net cash flow that is identical to the net cash flow for the lease obligation; that is, financial risk is neutralized. Such a loan, called an *equivalent loan*, is illustrated later. Fortunately, it has been mathematically demonstrated that rather than going through the time-consuming effort to construct an equivalent loan, all the decision-maker need do is discount the direct cash flow from leasing by an adjusted discount rate. The adjusted discount rate can be approximated by the following formula:[6]

---

[6] As noted by Brealey and Myers, *Principles of Corporate Finance*, "The direct cash flows are typically assumed to be *safe* flows that investors would discount at approximately the same rate as the interest and principal on a secured loan issued by the lessee" (p. 629). There is justification for applying a different discount rate to the various components of the direct cash flow from leasing.

Adjusted discount rate
    $= (1 - \text{Marginal tax rate}) \times (\text{Cost of borrowing money})$

The formula assumes that leasing will displace debt on a dollar-for-dollar basis.[7]

Given the direct cash flow from leasing and the adjusted discount rate, the NPV of the lease can be computed. We shall refer to the NPV of the lease as simply the *value of the lease*. A negative value for a lease indicates that leasing will not be more economically beneficial than borrowing to purchase. A positive value means that leasing will be more economically beneficial. However, leasing will be attractive only if the NPV of the asset assuming normal financing is positive *and* the value of the lease is positive, or if the sum of the NPV of the asset assuming normal financing and the value of the lease is positive.

In order to evaluate the direct cash flow from leasing for the machine considered by the Hieber Machine Shop Company in our previous illustration, we must know the firm's cost of borrowing money. Suppose that the cost of borrowing money has been determined to be 10%. The adjusted discount rate is then found by applying the formula:

$$\text{Adjusted discount rate} = (1 - 0.40) \times (0.10) = 0.06, \text{ or } 6\%$$

The adjusted discount rate of 6% is then employed to determine the value of the lease. The worksheet is shown as Exhibit 2. The value of the lease is −$448. Hence, from a purely economic point of view, the machine should be purchased by the Lysle Construction Company rather than leased. Recall that the NPV of the machine assuming normal financing is $11,540.

CONCEPT OF AN EQUIVALENT LOAN

The value of the lease considered by the Lysle Construction Company was shown to be −$448. Suppose the firm had the opportunity

---

[7] Brealey and Myers, *Principles of Corporate Finance*, p. 634. The formula must be modified, as explained later, if the lessee believes that leasing does not displace debt on dollar-for-dollar basis.

to obtain a $51,748 five-year loan at 10% interest with the follow-ing principal repayment schedule:[8]

End of year	0	1	2	3	4	5
Repayment	0	$8,757	$11,039	$11,450	$12,137	$8,365

(Recall that the firm's marginal borrowing rate was assumed to be 10%.)

Exhibit 3 shows the net cash flow for each year if the loan is used to purchase the machine. In addition to the loan, the firm must make an initial outlay of $7,652.

The net cash flow for each year if the machine is leased is also presented in Exhibit 3. Notice that the net cash flows of the two financing alternatives are equivalent, with the exception of year 0. Therefore, the loan presented above is called the *equivalent loan for the lease.*

We can now understand why borrowing to purchase is more economically attractive for Hieber Machine Shop Company. The equivalent loan produces the same net cash flow as the lease in all years after year 0. Hence, the equivalent loan has equalized the financial risk of the two financing alternatives. However, the net cash outlay in year 0 is $7,652 compared to $8,100 if the machine is leased. The difference, –$448, is the value of the lease. Notice that the lease valuation model produced the same value for the lease without constructing an equivalent loan.

Exhibit 2: Worksheet for Determining the Value of a Lease

End of year	Direct cash flow from leasing	Present value of $1 at 6%	Present value
0	$51,300	1.0000	$51,300
1	(11,862)	0.9434	(11,191)
2	(13,618)	0.8900	(12,120)
3	(13,367)	0.8396	(11,223)
4	(13,367)	0.7921	(10,588)
5	(8,867)	0.7473	(6,626)
Value (or NPV) of lease			$(448)

[8] The loan payments are determined by solving for the set of repayments and interest each period that would result in the value of purchase (accompanied by a loan) being equivalent to leasing.

Exhibit 3: Equivalent Loan for Lease versus Borrow-to-Buy Decision Faced by Hieber Machine Shop Company

Period	0	1	2	3	4	5
Leasing: Cash flows:						
– Lease payments	–$13,500	–$13,500	–$13,500	–$13,500	–$13,500	$0
+ Tax shield	5,400	5,400	5,400	5,400	5,400	0
Net cash flow	–$8,100	–$8,100	–$8,100	–$8,100	–$8,100	$0
Purchasing: Cash flows:						
– Purchase cost	–$66,000					$3,600
+ Tax credit	6,600					5,267
+ Residual value						
+ Depreciation tax-shield	0	$3,762	$5,518	$5,267	$5,267	
+ Loan	51,748					
– Principal repayment	0	–8,757	–11,039	–11,450	–12,137	–8,365
– Interest on loan	0	–5,175	–4,299	–3,195	–2,050	–836
+ Interest tax-shield	0	2,070	1,720	1,278	820	334
Net cash flow	–$7,652	–$8,100	–$8,100	–$8,100	–$8,100	$0
Loan account:						
Previous balance	$0	$51,748	$42,991	$31,953	$20,503	$8,365
Principal repayment (+ loan)	+51,748	–8,757	–11,039	–11,450	–12,137	–8,365
New balance	$51,748	$42,991	$31,953	$20,503	$8,365	$0
Value (NPV) of lease*	–$448					

* Difference between the net cash flows in year 0 [–8,100 – (–7,652)].

COMPARISON OF ALTERNATIVE LEASES

The potential lessee may have the opportunity to select from several leasing arrangements offered by the same lessor or different lessors. From a purely economic perspective, the potential lessor should select the leasing arrangement with the greatest positive value. This requires an analysis of the direct cash flow from leasing for each of the leasing arrangements available.

For example, suppose that a firm has two leasing arrangements available to lease a given asset. The direct cash flow from leasing is shown below for each alternative:

End of	Direct cash flow from leasing	
year	Lease 1	Lease 2
0	$42,000	$45,800
1	(15,000)	(13,000)
2	(15,000)	(16,000)
3	(15,000)	(18,000)
4	(1,000)	(4,000)

The value of the lease using an adjusted discount rate of 6% and 8% is summarized below:

Adjusted	Value of	
discount rate	Lease 1	Lease 2
6%	$1,109	$1,015
8	2,663	2,818

When the adjusted discount rate is 6%, both leases are economically beneficial. However, Lease 1 is marginally superior to Lease 2. The value of both leases increases when the adjusted discount rate is 8%. In this case, Lease 1 is slightly less attractive than Lease 2. The NPVs of both leases for discount rates ranging from 4% to 10% are shown in Exhibit 4.

ANOTHER APPROACH TO LEASE VALUATION

Rather than determining the net present value of a lease, many lessors use a different approach when attempting to demonstrate to potential lessees the economic attractiveness of a particular leasing arrangement. The approach is a comparison of the after-tax interest rate on the lease with the after-tax cost of borrowing money. The reason this approach appears to be popular is that management finds it easy to comprehend a rate concept but difficult to appreciate the net present value of a lease concept.

The after-tax interest rate on the lease is found by determining the discount rate that equates the direct cash flow from leasing to zero; that is, it is the discount rate that makes the value of the lease equal to zero.[9] This discount rate is also referred to as the *internal rate of return*. The after-tax interest rate on the lease is then compared to the after-tax cost of borrowing money. When the after-tax interest rate on the lease exceeds the after-tax cost of borrowing money, borrowing to purchase is more economical than leasing. Leasing is more economical when the after-tax cost of borrowing money is greater than the after-tax interest rate on the lease.

Exhibit 1 shows the direct cash flow from leasing for the lease arrangement available to the Hieber Machine Shop Company. To determine the after-tax interest rate on the lease, the direct cash flow from leasing is discounted at rates between 6.0% and 6.4% in Exhibit 5. The discount rate that produces a present value close to zero for the direct cash flow from leasing is 6.3%. Hence, the after-tax interest rate on the lease is about 6.3%.[10]

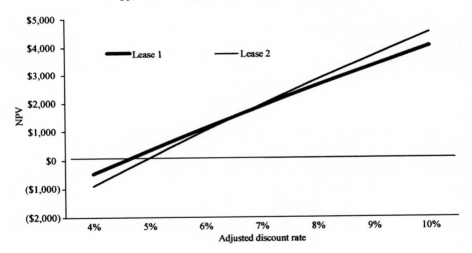

Exhibit 4: The NPV of Lease 1 and Lease 2 for Different Adjusted Discount Rates

[9] The procedure is identical to finding a yield on an investment or the effective interest cost on borrowed funds. The yield is the discount rate that equates the cash flow to the investment. The effective interest rate is the discount rate that equates the funds received in the initial period to the repayment of principal and interest over the term of the loan. The after-tax interest rate on the lease could have been stated in an analogous manner. The discount rate that equates the value of the lease to zero is the discount rate that equates the direct cash from leasing in the periods after the initial period to the direct cash flow from leasing in the initial period.

[10] The precise answer may be obtained using a financial calculator that has the IRR program or by using a spreadsheet program function, such as the IRR function in Microsoft's Excel.

Exhibit 5: Determination of After-Tax Interest Rate on the Lease

Year	Direct cash flow from leasing	PV at 6%	PV at 6.1%	PV at 6.2%	PV at 6.3%	PV at 6.4%
0	$51,300	$51,300	$51,300	$51,300	$51,300	$51,300
1	(11,862)	(11,191)	(11,180)	(11,169)	(11,159)	(11,148)
2	(13,618)	(12,120)	(12,097)	(12,074)	(12,052)	(12,029)
3	(13,367)	(11,223)	(11,191)	(11,160)	(11,128)	(11,097)
4	(13,367)	(10,588)	(10,548)	(10,508)	(10,469)	(10,429)
5	(8,867)	(6,626)	(6,594)	(6,563)	(6,533)	(6,502)
Value of lease		$(448)	$(310)	$(174)	$(41)	$95

When the after-tax cost of borrowing is 6%, the lease arrangement is not attractive. However, when the after-tax cost of borrowing money is 8%, the lease arrangement is attractive.

In the previous illustration, the determination that was made as to whether the lease was economically attractive was precisely the same determination that was made when the net present value lease valuation model was used. The identity of the result is not peculiar to this illustration. The two approaches will always produce the same result.

The advantage of the net present value lease valuation model presented is that it permits interaction of the investment and financing decisions. As a result it is simple to determine whether an investment proposal that has a negative net present value assuming normal financing can be made economically attractive by a favorable lease arrangement. With the after-tax interest on the lease approach, this is not done as easily. That approach requires management to revise its estimate of the cost of capital when the after-tax interest rate on the lease is less than the after-tax cost of borrowing money and then to reevaluate the investment proposal with the revised cost of capital. This is an extremely complicated and awkward approach since it requires a continuous revision of the cost of capital as attractive lease arrangements become available. No simple solution to this problem has been proffered in the literature.

The rate approach will not always provide the same solution as the net present value approach when lease arrangements are compared. Differences in the selection of the best lease arrangement may result when the number of advance payments is different, when the lease payments are not uniform, or when the tax credit is handled any differently.[11] The best lease arrangement is the one with the greatest NPV. Therefore, if conflicts arise when comparing lease arrangements by the two methods, the decision should be based on the NPV of the lease.

---

[11] The situation is analogous to conditions in which the yield technique in capital budgeting may produce rankings conflicting with those produced by the net present value technique.

Chapter 13

Uncertainty and the Lease Valuation Model

T he lease valuation model presented assumes that the appropriate discount rate that should be used to discount the direct cash flow from leasing is the after-tax cost of borrowed funds. However, when management believes that any components of the direct cash flow from leasing have a degree of risk different from that of the cash flows from borrowing, a different discount rate for each component is justified. Furthermore, the use of the after-tax cost of borrowed funds assumes that management believes that leasing displaces borrowing on a dollar-for-dollar basis. In this chapter these issues are examined. We also illustrate how management can test the sensitivity of the proposed solution to the lease valuation model to changes in the values assigned to factors in the model.

ALTERNATIVE DISCOUNT RATES AND THE UNCERTAINTY OF CASH FLOWS

In the lease valuation model presented, all components of the direct cash flow from leasing are discounted at the same discount rate, the adjusted discount rate. The adjusted discount rate is the after-tax cost of borrowing money. It is found by multiplying the cost of borrowing money by 1 minus the marginal tax rate. Yet there is theoretical justification for discounting some components of the direct cash flow at different discount rates.

In general, the discount rate applied to a cash flow should reflect the riskiness inherent in realizing the cash flow. The greater the risk, the greater is the discount rate that should be employed. If the cash flow is as risky as the cash flow from the firm's "average" project, then in the NPV analysis used in capital budgeting assuming normal financing, the appropriate rate is the firm's after-tax cost of capital.

184 Uncertainty and the Lease Valuation Model

However, when the cash flow is riskier than the cash flow from an "average" project, one approach to handle the uncertainty is to discount the *expected value of the cash flow* by the *risk-adjusted discount rate*. Two new concepts are introduced in the risk-adjusted discount rate approach. First, by expected value of the cash flow we mean the cash flow weighted by its likelihood of occurrence. For example, if there is a 50-50 chance of the after-tax proceeds from the sale of an asset being $2,000 or $5,200, then the expected value of the cash flow is $3,600.[1] Second, a risk-adjusted discount rate means that a premium is added to the after-tax cost of capital to discount the cash flow in capital budgeting analysis under normal financing and that a premium is added to the adjusted discount rate in valuing the lease. From a practical point of view, just how much of a premium is appropriate is often difficult to quantify.

As explained in Chapter 11, a pitfall of the risk-adjusted discount rate approach is that it lumps together in the valuation process the time value of money and risk attitudes, thereby resulting in the compounding of risk over time. Because of this drawback, another approach to the treatment of uncertainty is recommended within the context of NPV analysis. The approach is known as the *certainty equivalent approach* and was explained in Chapter 11. Whereas the risk-adjusted discount rate approach adjusts the discount rate, the certainty equivalent approach adjusts the cash flow in a special way. The certainty equivalent is the amount the decision-maker is willing to accept with certainty to forgo the risk of receiving the uncertain cash flow.[2] In essence the certainty equivalent converts the expected value of the cash flow into a cash flow that the decision maker is willing to accept with certainty.

---

[1] The expected value of the cash flow is found as follows: 0.6 times $2,000 + 0.6 times $6,200 = $3,600.

[2] Strictly speaking, it must be noted that to marry the certainty equivalent approach to the net present value rule, management must apply the approach in a manner that prices market risk and not individual attitudes toward risk. Recall that the foundation of the net present value rule is that it measures changes in market value and, therefore, the wealth position of the owners. Now if the certainty equivalent approach is to be used to measure changes in the net present value (and the market value) of the firm, then it must be based on market parameters and not individual (subjective) ones. Thus, a "market" certainty equivalent is needed, *not* the certainty equivalent reflective of the individual decision maker's risk aversion or personal position.

For example, suppose management believes there is a 50-50 chance of the after-tax proceeds from the residual value being $2,000 or $5,200. As noted before, the expected value is $3,600. To determine the certainty equivalent, management must estimate how much it is willing to accept with certainty rather than face the possible cash flow involved. That is, suppose management can enter into a contract now to sell the asset at a preestablished price when the firm expects to dispose of it. How much must that preestablished price be? If management is willing to accept $2,900, then $2,900 is the certainty equivalent of receiving $2,000 or $5,200 with a 50-50 chance.

Once the certainty equivalent of the cash flow has been determined, the certainty equivalent cash flow is discounted at the risk-free rate. The risk-free rate is the appropriate discount rate because there is no uncertainty, by definition, in the certainty equivalent cash flow. The risk-free rate is often measured by the rate on U.S. government obligations.

In practice, the risk-adjusted discount rate approach is probably more commonly employed. Many practitioners find it easier to determine a premium for the risk-adjusted discount rate than to estimate the certainty equivalent.

Because some of the components of the direct cash flow from leasing may be known with certainty, some financial theorists argue that the appropriate adjusted discount rate should be the after-tax risk-free rate. That is, the adjusted discount rate should be computed using the following formula:

Adjusted discount rate = (1 − Marginal tax rate) × (Risk-free rate)

The three components of the cash flow that may be known with certainty are the after-tax lease payments, the depreciation tax shield, and any tax credit. The lease payments constitute a fixed charge, and hence there is no uncertainty about the cash outflow. The depreciation tax shield can be used even though in some years there may be no taxable income generated by the asset under consideration. The depreciation tax shield can be used to offset income from other projects. Even if there is a net operating loss, the loss may be carried back for 3 years and forward for 15 years. Depending on management's expectations about future operations and the resulting tax liability, the probability of benefiting from uncertainty in such instances pertains to the timing, not the amount, of the tax benefits. The present value of the tax shield provided by depreciation then depends on when the benefits are included in the direct cash flow from leasing.

The effect of the discount rate selected on the outcome of the decision to lease or borrow to purchase can be analyzed by employing sensitivity analysis, which will be illustrated later in this section.

RESIDUAL VALUE AND THE LEASE TERM

If the residual value is anticipated by management to have a zero or trivial value at the end of the lease term, then the problems associated with discounting the residual value no longer exist. This suggests a way of coping with the treatment of the residual value. Management should select a lease term such that at the end of that term it expects the residual value to be insignificant.

The question then is, will there be a lessor willing to lease the asset for the length of time sought by the lessee? Within reasonable limits, there are lessors willing to bet that the asset will have a greater residual value than is expected by the lessee when the asset comes off-lease. Lease packagers are particularly helpful in finding lessors that believe more will be "left on the table" than lessees believe will be left.

DEBT DISPLACEMENT AND THE
LEASE VALUATION MODEL

When illustrating the lease valuation model previously it was always assumed that one dollar of leasing displaces one dollar of debt. Yet some managers believe that leasing can increase the firm's debt capacity. Although it is doubtful that management can continually fool lenders by using lease financing in lieu of debt financing, there may be certain circumstances in which a lease arrangement does not displace debt on a dollar-for-dollar basis.

When this occurs, the adjusted discount rate used to discount the direct cash flow from leasing must be modified. The adjusted discount rate, in general, is equal to:

Adjusted discount rate
= [1 − (Marginal tax rate × Debt displacement rate)]
  × Cost of borrowed funds

For example, if the cost of borrowed funds is 10% and $1 of leasing is assumed to displace only 60 cents of debt (that is, a debt displacement rate of 60%), the adjusted discount rate is

$$[1 - (0.40 \times 0.60)] \times 0.10 = 0.076, \text{ or } 7.6\%$$

In the model presented earlier in this chapter, we had the special case of the above formula when the debt displacement rate was 100%. When the debt displacement rate is less than 100%, the adjusted discount rate will increase. For example, the adjusted discount rate is 6% in the previous example when the debt displacement rate is 100%. Since the direct cash flow from leasing will be discounted at a higher adjusted discount rate as the debt displacement rate increases, the value of the lease will increase. This is illustrated later in this section.

SENSITIVITY ANALYSIS

It is not uncommon in economic models to find that the proposed solution is sensitive to changes in the factors of which the model is composed. The lease valuation model, for example, depends on the accuracy and certainty of such factors as the borrowing rate, the marginal tax rate, the timing of the tax shields, the estimated residual value, and the appropriate rate to discount the residual value and any additional operating expenses. The capital budgeting model assuming normal financing depends on additional factors that may not be known with certainty.

Uncertainty about the value that should be assigned to one or more factors in an economic model may reduce the confidence management has in the proposed solution generated by the model. To assist management when the values of one or more factors are uncertain, sensitivity analysis can be employed. In sensitivity analysis the values of the factors not known with certainty are altered to assess the effect, if any, such changes will have on the proposed solution. The following illustrations based on the Hieber Machine Shop Company lease-or-borrow-to-buy decision demonstrate how sensitivity analysis may be useful for the lease versus borrow-to-purchase decision.[3]

The direct cash flow from leasing used to illustrate the lease valuation model was:

Year	0	1	2	3	4	5
Direct cash flow from leasing	$51,300	($11,862)	($13,618)	($13,367)	($13,367)	($8,867)

To determine the sensitivity of the value of the lease to changes in the adjusted discount rate, the direct cash flow from leasing is discounted using different borrowing rates. Exhibit 1 reports the value of the lease for borrowing rates ranging between 5% and 25%. Assuming a marginal tax rate of 40%, which was assumed in computing the direct cash flow from leasing, the cost of borrowing associated with each adjusted discount rate is also shown in Exhibit 1.

The value of the lease increases as higher adjusted discount rates are applied. The value of the lease ranges from −$4,811 to $9,848. The adjusted discount rate at which management would be indifferent between leasing and borrowing to buy is the rate at which the value of the lease is zero. From Exhibit 1 it can be seen that the value of the lease changes from a negative value to a positive value when the borrowing rate is approximately 10.5%. Hence, the break-even adjusted discount rate is between 6.25% and 6.5%. The precise break-even adjusted discount rate is 6.33%, which corresponds to a borrowing rate of 6.33%/0.6 = 10.55%. This means that if the cost of borrowing to the Hieber Machine Shop Company is between 10.42% and 10.83%, the company would be indifferent between leasing and borrowing to buy.

---

[3] Although the illustrations are within the context of the net present value lease valuation model, sensitivity analysis can be used if the after-tax interest rate on the lease approach is employed. The uncertainty usually focuses on the residual value. An after-tax interest rate on the lease is then computed for different possible residual values expected by the lessee.

Exhibit 1: Sensitivity of the Value of a Lease to Changes in the Adjusted Discount Rate

At 6.33%, the value of the lease is zero. Therefore, 6.33% is the break-even adjusted discount rate.

Borrowing rate = Adjusted discount rate / 0.60

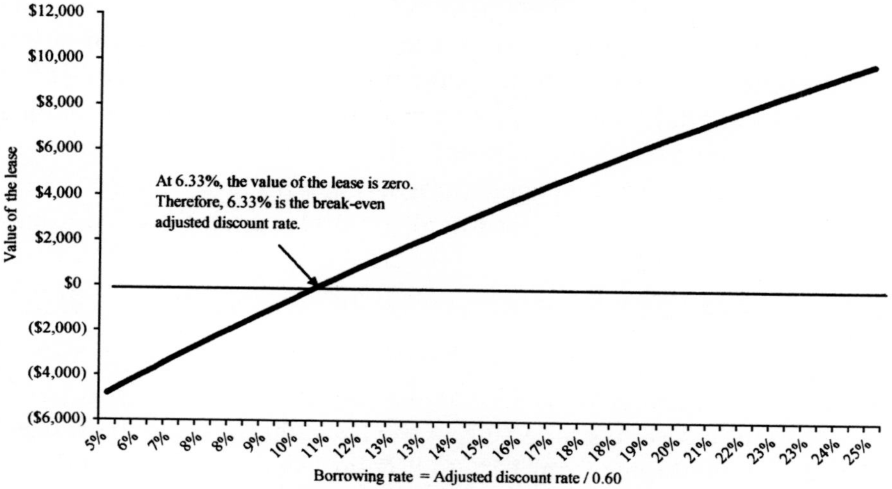

Notice that when the sensitivity analysis technique is used to determine when the value of the lease is zero (that is, the indifference rate between leasing and borrowing to purchase), this point is the after-tax interest rate on the lease. Recall that the after-tax interest rate on the lease is the discount rate that equates the present value of the direct cash flow from leasing to zero. For the leasing arrangement under consideration by Hieber Machine Shop Company, it was shown that the rate was 6.33%.

Suppose instead that Hieber Machine Shop Company's management does not believe that leasing displaces debt on a dollar-for-dollar basis. It believes that leasing does use up debt capacity, but it is not certain of the amount displaced.

To determine the sensitivity of the value of the lease to the percentage of debt displaced by leasing, the direct cash flow from leasing is discounted using debt displacement rates between 0% and 100%, at 10% increments. It is assumed that the cost of borrowed funds is 10% and that the marginal tax rate is 40%. The results are shown in Exhibit 2.

The value of the lease becomes more attractive as the amount of debt assumed to be displaced by the lease decreases. If management believes that leasing displaces less than about 90% of debt, then leasing is more economical.

Now suppose management is uncertain about the estimated residual value of $3,600 it expects to realize five years from now if the machine is purchased. Management has estimated the firm's after-tax cost of capital to be 14%. The risk associated with the residual value is greater than that of the cash flows associated with the firm's "average" project. Yet management is not certain how much riskier.

Management has determined the direct cash flow from leasing to be as follows:

Year	0	1	2	3	4	5
Direct cash flow from leasing	$51,300	($11,862)	($13,618)	($13,367)	($13,367)	($5,267)

Without the residual value of $3,600, the cash flow in year 5 is −$5,267.

Exhibit 3 shows the value of the lease discounting the residual value at discount rates from 14% to 20% at 1% increments, while discounting the other components of the direct cash flow from leasing at 6%. The greater the uncertainty about the residual value, the more economically attractive is the lease alternative. In our example, leasing is attractive for any discount rate greater than or equal to 17%.

Exhibit 2: Sensitivity of the Value of a Lease to the Amount of Debt Displaced by Leasing

Debt displacement rate (%)	Adjusted discount rate (%)*	Value of lease ($)
0	10.0	4,583
10	9.6	4,116
20	9.2	3,641
30	8.8	3,159
40	8.4	2,669
50	8.0	2,170
60	7.6	1,664
70	7.2	1,149
80	6.8	626
90	6.4	93
100	6.0	−448

* Assuming that the marginal tax rate is 40% and that the cost of borrowed funds is 10%, the adjusted discount rate is:

[1 − (Debt displacement rate × 0.40)] × 0.10

Exhibit 3: Sensitivity of the Value of a Lease to the Estimated Residual Value

Discount rate for residual value (%)	Value of lease when other components of direct cash flow from leasing are discounted at an adjusted rate of	
	6.0%*	4.8%**
14	$373	−$1,149
15	453	−1,069
16	529	−993
17	601	−921
18	669	−853
19	734	−788
20	796	−726

* The adjusted discount rate assuming a borrowing rate of 10% and a marginal tax rate of 40%.
** The adjusted discount rate assuming a risk-free rate of 8% and a marginal tax rate of 40%.

Suppose management believes that although the residual value is uncertain, there is absolutely no uncertainty about the tax shields and the tax credit associated with the direct cash flow from leasing. Management has estimated the risk-free rate to be 8% and, as noted above, the after-tax cost of capital to be 14%.

Exhibit 3 shows the value of the lease when 4.8% (8% times 1 minus a 40% marginal tax rate) is used to discount the direct cash flow from leasing, excluding the residual value. The latter component is discounted at the various rates shown in Exhibit 3. Assuming the discount rates represent a reasonable range within which to discount the residual value, it can be seen that the leasing arrangement will never be more economically attractive in this case.

Chapter 14

Generalization of the Lease Valuation Model

The lease valuation model we presented in Chapter 12 is appropriate when the firm anticipates that it can fully absorb the expenses associated with either financing alternative as they arise. In this chapter we present an extension of the lease valuation model. The model is appropriate for a firm currently in a nontaxpaying position but believes it will commence paying taxes at some specified future date.

Julian Franks and Stewart Hodges extended the lease valuation model formulated by Professor Myers.[1] The model is generalized to cover the case where a firm is currently in a nontaxpaying position but expects to resume paying taxes at a specific future date. Expenses in the nontaxpaying years are assumed to be carried forward as tax losses. This tax benefit, along with any tax credit, which can also be carried forward, is then assumed to be absorbed in a single year. The extended model is useful because many firms considering leasing are, or expect to be, in such a position.

The procedure to compute the value of the lease is considerably more complicated in such cases. This procedure is explained and illustrated below.

ASSUMPTIONS AND NOTATION

The following assumptions and notation are employed in calculating the value of the lease:

---

[1] See Julian R. Franks and Stewart D. Hodges, "Valuation of Financial Lease Contracts: A Note," *Journal of Finance* (May 1978): 657–69. The mathematical representation of the model is offered in footnote 3 (pages 666–67) of their article. The explanation of how to compute the value of the lease and the extension to consider any tax credit and the residual value are our own.

1. Year H is the last year of cash flow consequences.
2. The firm is currently in a nontaxpaying position.
3. The firm expects to resume paying taxes in year G (where G is less than or equal to H), having a "tax holiday" from year 0 to year $G - 1$.
4. The firm will pay taxes from year G to year H at the same marginal tax rate.
5. All expenses incurred during the "tax holiday" are carried forward as tax losses and *fully* absorbed in year G.
6. Any tax credit is carried forward and fully utilized in year G.

VALUING THE LEASE

Using the following 14 steps, the value of the lease can be determined.

Step 1: Compute the present value of the lease payments from year 0 to year $G - 1$ at the pretax borrowing rate.

Step 2: Compute the present value of the sum of the (1) after-tax lease payment, (2) depreciation tax shield, (3) any tax credit, and (4) lost residual value for years G through H at the after-tax borrowing rate. When discounting, treat year G as year 0.

Step 3: Compute the difference between the depreciation tax shield and the lease payment tax shield for the years 0 through $G - 1$. Add up these differences.

Step 4: Add up the amounts computed in Step 2 and Step 3.

Step 5: Find the present value of the amount in Step 4 for G years using the pretax borrowing rate.

Step 6: For years 1 through $G - 1$, multiply the lease payment

1 − [Present value of $1 using the pretax borrowing rate for t years]

where t corresponds to the year and varies from 1 to $G - 1$.

Step 7: Sum for years 1 through $G - 1$ the amounts computed in Step 6.

Step 8: Multiply the amount in Step 4 by

1 − [Present value of $1 using the pretax borrowing rate for G years]

Step 9: Add the amounts computed in Step 7 and Step 8.
Step 10: Divide the sum in Step 9 by

1 – (Marginal tax rate)
 [1 – Present value of $1 using the pretax borrowing rate for *G* years]

Step 11: Multiply the amount in Step 10 by the marginal tax rate.
Step 12: Compute the present value of the amount in Step 11 using the pretax borrowing rate for *G* years.
Step 13: Add the amounts in Step 1, Step 5, and Step 12.
Step 14: Subtract from the purchase cost the amount computed in Step 13. The result is the value (NPV) of the lease.

Let's apply the generalized lease valuation model to the lease considered by the Hieber Machine Shop Company in Chapter 12 assuming the firm is currently in a nontaxpaying position but anticipates commencing tax payments in year 3 (that is, *G* = 3). All tax benefits are assumed to be carried forward and fully absorbed in year 3.

Step 1: Compute the present value of the lease payments from year 0 to year 2 at 10%. Since $13,500 is paid in each year, the present value is

PV of lease payments for years 0 through 2
 = $13,500[PV of $1 of an annuity due for three years at 10%]
 = $13,500[2.7355] = $36,930

Step 2: Compute the present value of the sum of the (1) after-tax lease payment, (2) depreciation tax shield, (3) tax credit, and (4) lost residual value for years 3 to 5 using a 6% discount rate. For discounting purposes, treat year 3 as year 0.

Year	After-tax lease payment	Depreciation tax-shield	Tax credit	Residual	Total
3	$8,100	$5,267	$6,600	$0	$19,967
4	8,100	5,267	0	0	13,367
5	0	5,267	0	3,600	8,867

Computation of present value of these cash flows as of the end of year 3:

Year	For discounting purposes	Total	PV of $1 at 6%	PV
3	0	$19,967	1.0000	$19,967
4	1	13,367	0.9434	12,610
5	2	8,867	0.8900	7,892
			Total	$40,469

Step 3: Compute the difference between the depreciation tax shield and the lease payment tax shield for years 0 to 2. Add these differences.

Year	Depreciation tax-shield	Lease payment tax-shield	Difference
0	$0	$5,400	−$5,400
1	3,762	5,400	−1,638
2	5,518	5,400	118
		Total	−$6,920

Step 4: Add the amounts computed in Step 2 and Step 3.

$40,469 + (−$6,920) = $33,549

Step 5: Find the present value of the amount in Step 4 for three years using 10%.

$33,549[PV of $1 three years from now at 10%]
    = $33,549(0.7513) = $25,205

Step 6: For years 1 and 2 multiply the lease payment by
1 − [PV of $1 for t years at 10%]

Year	Lease payment	PV of $1	1 − PV of $1	Lease payment times (1 − PV of $1)
1	$13,500	$0.9091	$0.0909	$1,227
2	13,500	0.8264	0.1736	2,344

Step 7: Sum for years 1 and 2 the amounts computed in Step 6.

$1,227 + $2,344 = $3,571

Step 8: Multiply the amount in Step 4 by

1 − [PV of $1 for three years]

$33,549[1 − 0.7513] = $8,344

Step 9: Add the amounts in Step 7 and Step 8.

$3,571 + $8,344 = $11,915

Step 10: Divide the sum in Step 9 by

1 – 0.4[1 – PV of $1 for three years at 10%]
$11,915/(1 – 0.4[1 – 0.7513])
= $11,915/0.9005 = $13,232

Step 11: Multiply the amount in Step 10 by 0.4.

0.4($13,232) = $5,293

Step 12: Compute the present value of the amount in Step 11 for three years at 10%.

$5,293[PV of $1 for three years at 10%]
$5,293(0.7513) = $3,977

Step 13: Add the amounts in Step 1, Step 5, and Step 12.

$36,930 + $25,205 + $3,977 = $66,112

Step 14: Subtract from the purchase cost the amount computed in Step 13.

$66,000 – $66,112 = –$112

The value (NPV) of the lease is –$112. When it is assumed that the tax shields and the tax credit could be fully utilized at the time of recognition, the value of the lease is –$448.

VALUATION WHEN THERE ARE LIMITATIONS ON CARRY FORWARD ITEMS

The generalized model assumes that the entire tax-shield can be carried forward and fully absorbed in a single year. There are limitations as to the number of years a tax loss and any tax credit may be carried forward. The model can accommodate this situation by modifying the following four steps to allow for tax losses that may be carried forward from year F to year G:

Step 3: Compute the difference between the depreciation tax shield and the lease tax shield for *years F through G* $-$ 1. Add up these differences.

Step 6: For year F' through year G $-$ 1, multiply the lease payment by

1 $-$ [Present value of $1 using the pretax borrowing rate for $(t - F' + 1)$ years]

where F' is the greater of 1 and F^2 and t varies from F' to $G - 1$.

Step 8: Multiply the amount in Step 4 by

1 $-$ [Present value of $1 using the pretax borrowing rate for
    $(G - F' + 1)$ years]

Step 10: Divide the value in Step 9 by

1 $-$ (Marginal tax rate)
    $\times$ [1 $-$ Present value of $1 using the pretax borrowing rate for
    $(G - F' + 1)$ years]

To illustrate how the model can be used when some of the tax-shields cannot be carried forward, let's change the tax law. Suppose Hieber Machine Shop Company is currently in a nontaxpaying position but expects to resume paying taxes in year 4. The tax credit cannot be carried forward, but tax losses in years 2 and 3 can be.

The value of the lease is $1,372, as shown below.

Step 1: Compute the present value of the lease payments from year 0 to year 3 at 10%. Since $13,500 is paid in each year, the present value is

$13,500[PV of $1 of an annuity due for four years at 10%]
$13,500[1 + 2.4869] = $47,073

---

[2] For example, if F is year 5, then F$'$ is 5 since it is greater than 1. If F is 0, then F$'$ is 1 since 1 is greater than 0. Note that when F is zero, we have the case where all tax benefits can be carried forward.

Step 2: Compute the present value of the sum of the (1) after-tax lease payment, (2) depreciation tax-shield, (3) tax credit, and (4) lost residual value for years 4 and 5 using a 6% discount rate. For discounting purposes, treat year 4 as year 0.

Year	After-tax lease payment	Depreciation tax-shield	Tax credit	Residual	Total
4	$8,100	$5,267	$0	$0	$13,367
5	0	5,267	0	3,600	8,867

Computation of present value:

Year	For discounting purposes	Total	PV of $1 at 6%	PV
4	0	$13,367	$1.0000	$13,367
5	1	8,867	0.9434	8,365
Total				$21,732

Step 3: Compute the difference between the depreciation tax shield and the lease payment tax shield for years 2 and 3. Add these differences.

Year	Depreciation tax-shield	Lease payment tax-shield	Difference
2	$5,518	$5,400	$118
3	5,267	5,400	−133
		Total	−$15

Step 4: Add the amounts computed in Step 2 and Step 3.

$21,732 + (−15) =$ 21,717

Step 5: Find the present value of the amount in Step 4 for four years at 10%.

$21,717[PV of $1 four years from now at 10%]
$21,717(0.6830) = $14,833

Step 6: For years 2 and 3, multiply the lease payment by

1 − [PV of $1 for $(t − 2 + 1)$ years at 10%]

Year	For discounting $(t − 2 + 1)$	Lease payment	PV of $1	1 − PV of $1 at 6%	Lease payment times (1 − PV of $1)
2	1	$13,500	$0.9091	$0.0909	$1,227
3	2	13,500	0.8264	0.1736	2,344

Step 7: Sum for years 2 and 3 the amounts computed in Step 6.

$1,227 + $2,344= $3,571

Step 8: Multiply the amount in Step 4 by

1 − [PV of $1 for (4 − 2 + 1) years at 10%]
$21,717(1 − 0.7513) = $5,401

Step 9: Add the amounts in Step 7 and Step 8.

$3,571 + $5,401 = $8,972

Step 10: Divide the value in Step 9 by

1 − 0.4[1 − PV of $1 for (4 − 2 + 1) years at 10%]
$8,972/(1 − 0.4[1 − 0.7513])
$8,972/0.9005 = $9,963

Step 11: Multiply the amount in Step 10 by 0.4.

0.4($9,963) − $3,985

Step 12: Compute the present value of the amount in Step 11 for four years at 10%.

$3,985[PV of $1 for four years at 10%] = $3,985(0.6830) = $2,722

Step 13: Add the amounts in Step 1, Step 5, and Step 12.

$47,073 + $14,833 + $2,722 = $64,628

Step 14: Subtract from the purchase cost the amount computed in Step 13.

$66,000 − $64,628 = $1,372

Because Lysle Construction loses the tax credit and cannot carry all tax losses forward, leasing has become attractive. The value of the lease is now $1,372 compared to −$448 when all tax benefits are fully absorbed as they arise and −$112 when all the tax benefits can be carried forward and fully absorbed in a single year by a firm currently in a nontaxpaying position.

VALUATION WHEN NO TAX BENEFITS ARE EXPECTED

For a firm that is currently in a nontaxpaying position and does not expect to receive any of the tax benefits, the value of the lease is easier to compute. The following two steps provide the value of the lease.

Step 1: Compute the present value of the sum of the (1) lease payments, and (2) lost residual value before taxes at the pretax borrowing rate.

Step 2: Subtract from the purchase cost the amount computed in Step 1.

To illustrate, suppose the management of Hieber Machine Shop Company is not presently paying taxes and does not expect to receive any tax benefits associated with either financing alternative. Applying the above two steps, the value of the lease is $5,981, as shown below:

Step 1:

Present value of the lease payments at 10%:

$13,500[PV of $1 of an annuity due for five years at 10%]
    = $13,500[1 + 3.1699] = $56,294

Present value of the residual value before taxes:

$6,000[PV of $1 for five years at 10%] = $6,000(0.6209) = $3,725

Total present value = $56,294 + $3,725 = $60,019

Step 2:

Value of lease = $66,000 − $60,019 = $5,981

Questions for Section IV

1. How does the analysis of a borrow-to-buy versus lease decision differ when analyzing a net lease versus a gross lease?

2. What are the direct cash flows from leasing? What factors in the buy and leasing decision affect the direct cash flows?

3. Why are lost depreciation shields included in the analysis of the direct cash flows from leasing?

4. What is the equivalent loan in the context of the borrow-to-buy versus leasing decision?

5. How does the assumption of the debt-displacement of leasing affect the discount rate used in the leasing analysis?

6. Suppose that in the analysis of the buy-versus-lease decision the value of the lease is zero. How does one interpret a zero value for a lease?

7. In the analysis of the leasing decision, an assumption is made about the use of deductions for tax purposes. What is this assumption and how is the analysis altered if this assumption is not valid?

Problems for Section IV

1. The Misthosi Company is considering the acquisition of a machine that costs $50,000 if bought today. The company can buy or lease the machine. If it buys the machine, the machine would be depreciated as a 3-year MACRS asset and is expected to have a salvage value of $1,000 at the end of the 5-year useful life. If leased, the lease payments are $12,000 each year for four years, payable at the beginning of each year. The marginal tax rate of Mishthosi is 30% and its cost of capital is 10%. Assume that the lease is a net lease, that any tax benefits are realized in the year of the expense, and that there is no investment tax credit.

   MACRS rates of depreciation on a 3-year asset:

Year	Rate
1	33.33%
2	44.45%
3	14.81%
4	7.41%

   a. Calculate the depreciation for each year in the case of the purchase of this machine
   b. Calculate the direct cash flows from leasing initially and for each of the five years
   c. Calculate the adjusted discount rate
   d. Calculate the NPV of the lease

2. The Mietet Company is considering the acquisition of a machine that costs $1,000,000 if bought today. The company can buy or lease the machine. If it buys the machine, the machine would be depreciated as a 3-year MACRS asset and is expected to have a salvage value of $10,000 at the end of the 5-year useful life. If leased, the lease payments are $250,000 each year for four years, payable at the beginning of each year. Mietet's marginal tax rate is 35% and the cost of capital is 12%. Use the MACRS rates as provided in Problem 1. Assume that the lease is a net lease, that any tax benefits are realized in the year of the expense, and that there is no investment tax credit.

a. Calculate the depreciation for each year in the case of the purchase of this machine
b. Calculate the direct cash flows from leasing initially and for each of the five years
c. Calculate the adjusted discount rate
d. Calculate the NPV of the lease

3. The Rendilegping Company is considering the acquisition of a machine that costs $100,000 if bought today. The company can buy or lease the machine. If it buys the machine, the machine would be depreciated as a 3-year MACRS asset and is expected to have a salvage value of $5,000 at the end of the 5-year useful life. If leased, the lease payments are $24,000 each year for four years, payable at the beginning of each year. The marginal tax rate of the Rendilegping Company is 30% and the cost of capital is 15%. Use the MACRS rates as provided in Problem 1 and assume that the lease is a net lease, that any tax benefits are realized in the year of the expense, and that there is no investment tax credit.

a. Calculate the depreciation for each year in the case of the purchase of this machine
b. Calculate the direct cash flows from leasing initially and for each of the five years
c. Calculate the adjusted discount rate
d. Calculate the NPV of the lease
e. Calculate the amortization of the equivalent loan

4. The Arrende Corporation is considering the acquisition of a machine that costs $73,000 if bought today. The company can buy or lease the machine. If it buys the machine, the machine would be depreciated using the straight-line method, depreciating the full asset cost over five years, and is expected to have a salvage value of $2,000 at the end of the 5-year useful life. If leased, the lease payments are $17,500 each year for four years, payable at the beginning of each year. Arrende's marginal tax rate is 38% and the appropriate cost of capital is 10%. Assume that the lease is a net lease, that any tax benefits are realized in the year of the expense, and that there is no investment tax credit.

a. Calculate the depreciation for each year in the case of the purchase of this machine
b. Calculate the direct cash flows from leasing initially and for each of the five years
c. Calculate the adjusted discount rate
d. Calculate the NPV of the lease
e. Calculate the amortization of the equivalent loan

5. The Baillat Corporation is considering the acquisition of a machine that costs $89,000 if bought today. Baillat can buy or lease the machine. If it buys the machine, the machine would be depreciated as a 3-year MACRS asset and is expected to have a salvage value of $2,000 at the end of the 4-year useful life. If leased, the lease payments are $21,000 each year for four years, payable at the beginning of each year. Use the MACRS rates as provided in Problem 1 and assume that the lease is a net lease, that any tax benefits are realized in the year of the expense, and that there is no investment tax credit.

a. Calculate the NPV of the lease assuming a marginal tax rate is 30% and a cost of capital of 10%
b. Calculate the NPV of the lease assuming a marginal tax rate is 40% and a cost of capital of 10%
c. Calculate the NPV of the lease assuming a marginal tax rate is 30% and a cost of capital of 15%

Appendix

The Fundamentals of Equipment Leasing

In order to compare leasing with other methods of financing, it is necessary to understand the basics of how leasing works and the differences among the general categories of equipment leases. We cover this in this appendix along with (1) a critical evaluation of the reasons often cited for leasing, (2) the factors that should be considered in selecting a lessor, and (3) the various types of lease programs available.

BACKGROUND

A lease is a contract wherein, over the term of the lease, the lessor (owner) permits the lessee (user) the use of an asset in exchange for a promise by the latter to pay a series of lease payments. Most corporate financial executives recognize that earnings are derived from the use of an asset, not its ownership, and that leasing is simply an alternative financing method. While this recognition seems axiomatic today, it was not always a belief shared by financial executives. Except for the transportation industry, where leasing had long been employed for railroad rolling stock, until the 1970s the ownership ethic dominated equipment financing decisions. Leasing was regarded as a last resort form of financial transaction that prestigious and financially strong companies simply did not undertake.

HOW LEASING WORKS

A typical leasing transaction works as follows. The user-lessee first decides on the equipment needed. The lessee then decides on the

---

This appendix is adapted from Chapters 1 and 16 in Peter K. Nevitt and Frank J. Fabozzi, *Equipment Leasing* (New Hope, PA: Frank J. Fabozzi Associates, 2000).

manufacturer, the make, and the model. The lessee specifies any special features desired, the terms of warranties, guaranties, delivery, installation, and services. The lessee also negotiates the price. After the equipment and terms have been specified and the sales contract negotiated, the lessee enters into a lease agreement with the lessor. The lessee negotiates with the lessor on the length of the lease; the rental; whether sales tax, delivery, and installation charges should be included in the lease; and other optional considerations.

After the lease has been signed, the lessee assigns its purchase rights to the lessor, which then buys the equipment exactly as specified by the lessee. When the property is delivered, the lessee formally accepts the equipment to make sure it gets exactly what was ordered. The lessor then pays for the equipment, and the lease goes into effect. Rentals are usually net to the leasing company. Except in short-term operating leases, discussed later, taxes, service, insurance, and maintenance are the responsibility of the lessee and may not be deducted from rentals.

At the end of the lease term, the lessee usually has the option to renew the lease, to buy the equipment, or to terminate the agreement and return the equipment. As we shall see in later chapters, the options available to the lessee at the end of the lease are very significant in that the dimensions of such options determine the nature of the lease for tax purposes and the classification of the lease for financial accounting purposes.

When all costs associated with the use of the equipment are to be paid by the lessee and not included in the lease payments, the lease is called a *net lease* or *triple net lease*. Examples of such costs are property taxes, insurance, and maintenance. Most long-term lease financing transactions are net leases.

TYPES OF EQUIPMENT LEASES

Equipment leases fall into three general categories, each with a different type of purchase option.

1. *Non–tax-oriented leases* (also called *conditional sale leases, leases intended as security, hire-purchase leases, money-*

over-money leases, and *synthetic leases*), which either have nominal purchase options or automatically pass title to the lessee at the end of the lease.

2. *Tax-oriented true leases* (also sometimes called *guideline leases*), which either contain no purchase option or have a purchase option based on fair market value. There are two types of tax-oriented true leases: *single-investor leases* (also called *direct leases*) and *leveraged leases*.

3. *Tax-oriented TRAC leases for licensed over-the-road vehicles* (also called *open-end leases*), which have terminal rental adjustment clauses that shift the entire residual risk to the lessee but may permit the lessee to acquire the equipment at a fixed price at the end of the lease.

The Non–Tax-Oriented Lease or Conditional Sale Lease

A conditional sale lease transfers all incidents of ownership of the leased property to the lessee and usually gives the lessee a fixed price bargain purchase option or renewal option not based on fair market value at the time of exercise. Although generally the lessee has both legal title and tax title in a conditional sale lease, the tax rules and legal rules for determining when a lease constitutes a true lease or conditional sale are not always the same. Conditional sale leases for tax purposes may include leases for a lease term of more than 80% of the original useful life of the leased property or for a term whereby the estimated fair market value of the leased property at the end of the lease term is less than 20% of the original cost. The lessee under a conditional sale lease treats the property as owned on its balance sheet, depreciates the property for tax purposes, claims any tax credit which may be available, and deducts the interest portion of rent payments for tax purposes.[1] The lessor under a condi-

---

[1] A synthetic lease is a specialized type of conditional sale lease in which the lessee achieves operating lease treatment (off balance sheet) for accounting purposes, while retaining tax benefits. The lessor receives no tax benefits and has a security interest in the asset. Synthetic leases are discussed in Chapter 4 in Peter K. Nevitt and Frank J. Fabozzi, *Equipment Leasing* (New Hope, PA: Frank J. Fabozzi Associates, 2000).

tional sale lease treats the transaction as a loan and cannot offer the low lease rates associated with a true lease since the lessor does not retain the ownership tax benefits.

Equipment financing offered by vendors is often in the form of conditional sale leases. Most leasing done outside the United States is structured similarly to a conditional sale lease, although the tax implications may not be the same as in the United States.

The Tax-Oriented True Leases

The true lease offers all of the primary benefits commonly attributed to leasing. Substantial cost savings can often be achieved through the use of tax-oriented true leases in which the lessor claims and retains the tax benefits of ownership and passes through to the lessee most of such tax benefits in the form of reduced lease payments. The lessor claims tax benefits resulting from equipment ownership such as MACRS depreciation deductions, and the lessee deducts the full lease payment as an expense. The lessor in a true lease owns the leased equipment at the end of the lease term.

The principal advantage to a lessee of using a true lease to finance an equipment acquisition is the economic benefit that comes from the indirect realization of tax benefits that might otherwise be lost.

If the lessee is unable to generate a sufficient tax liability to currently use fully tax benefits, such as MACRS tax depreciation associated with equipment ownership, the cost of owning new equipment will effectively be higher than leasing the equipment under a true lease. Under these conditions leasing is usually a less costly alternative because the lessor uses the tax benefits from the acquisition and passes on most of these benefits to the lessee through a lower lease payment.

There are two categories of true leases: *single-investor leases* (or *direct leases*) and *leveraged leases*. Single-investor leases are essentially two-party transactions, with the lessor purchasing the leased equipment with its own funds and being at risk for 100% of the funds used to purchase the equipment. In a leveraged lease, on the other hand, there are three parties to the transaction: a lessee, a lessor (equity participant), and a long-term lender. In a leveraged lease the lessor provides only a portion of the purchase price of the leased equipment from its own funds (typically 20% to 25%), borrows the remainder of the purchase price (typically 75% to 80%) from third-party lenders on a nonrecourse basis, claims tax benefits associated with equipment ownership on 100% of the purchase price, and receives 100% of the residual value subject to any fixed price purchase options at fair market value or higher. The leveraged use of tax benefits and profit from the residual value constitutes the "leverage" in a leveraged lease. The greater benefits to the lessor enable the lessor to pass through greater benefits indirectly to the lessee in the form of reduced rents. At the end of this appendix we provide the fundamentals of leveraged leasing.

The lower cost of leasing realized by a lessee throughout the lease term in a true lease must be weighted against the loss of the leased asset's residual value at the end of the lease term. A framework for evaluating the tax and timing effects is presented in Chapter 12. In an absolute sense, the give-up of residual value is of small significance as long as the lessor assumes a realistic residual value for pricing purposes, the lease term constitutes a substantial portion of the economic life of the asset, and renewal options permit continuity of control for its economic life.

The Internal Revenue Service is well aware that parties to a lending transaction may find it more advantageous from a tax point of view to characterize an agreement as a "lease" rather than as a conditional sales agreement. Therefore, guidelines have been established by the IRS to distinguish between a true lease and a conditional sales agreement.[2]

TRAC Leases

The Deficit Reduction Act of 1984 authorized a new type of lease for over-the-road motor vehicles called a *TRAC lease* that combined the benefits of a true lease and a conditional sale. The name TRAC lease is derived from the fact that a TRAC lease contains a "terminal rental adjustment clause." Properly structured, a TRAC lease can be used to provide a lessee with true tax-oriented lease rates even though the lease contains a terminal rental adjustment clause which is comparable to a fixed-price purchase option.

---

[2] These guidelines are discussed in Chapter 5 in Nevitt and Fabozzi, *Equipment Leasing.*

TRAC leases can be used to finance motor vehicles used in a trade or business. While the statute is not entirely clear on the subject, the term motor vehicles most likely includes only motor vehicles such as trucks, truck tractors and trailer rigs, automobiles, and buses. On the other hand, vehicles such as farm tractors, construction equipment, and forklifts are probably not eligible for TRAC leases.

FULL PAYOUT LEASES

Thus far, the leases we have discussed are comparable to equipment financing transactions in that the lease term is for a substantial portion of the economic life of the leased equipment. In these leases the lessor expects to recover its entire investment plus (1) a desired yield or return on its investment from the rental stream payable under the lease, (2) any tax benefits the lessor is entitled to receive, and (3) the residual value the lessor anticipates receiving when the lease terminates. These types of leases are called *full payout leases*. Such leases are essentially financing transactions.

OPERATING LEASES

Other types of leases, called *operating leases*, in contrast, are not financing transactions. Operating leases may be for only a fraction of the life of the asset. The name is derived from the fact that it originally described a lease in which equipment was furnished along with an operator on a lease service arrangement, as, for example, with a piece of construction equipment, a ship, or an airplane.

An operating lease is always a true lease for tax purposes. That is, the lessor is entitled to all the tax benefits associated with ownership, and the lessee is entitled to deduct the rental payments.

Historically in the equipment leasing business the term operating lease was used fairly exclusively to describe short-term leases for a small fraction of the economic life of an asset. When FASB Statement No. 13 was enacted, it adopted that term as an accounting definition for leases with lease terms equal to as much as 75% of the economic life of the leased asset. This definition blurred the traditional difference between finance type leases and operating leases.

There is a specific meaning for leases classified as an operating lease for financial accounting purposes. Transactions classified as operating leases are not disclosed in the body of the balance sheet as financial obligations. Instead, they are shown in the footnotes to the financial statement as fixed obligations. This classification may arise despite the fact that the transaction is to all intents and purposes a financing transaction.

REASONS FOR LEASING

Leasing is an alternative to purchasing. Since the lessee is obligated to make a series of payments, a lease arrangement resembles a debt contract. Thus, the advantages cited for leasing are often based on a comparison between leasing and purchasing using borrowed funds on an intermediate-term (maturity between 3 and 10 years) or long-term (maturity greater than 10 years) basis.

Cost

Many lessees find true leasing attractive because of its apparent low cost. This is particularly evident where a lessee cannot currently use tax benefits associated with equipment ownership due to such factors as lack of currently taxable income, net operating loss carryforwards, or being subject to the alternative minimum tax.

If it were not for the different tax treatment for owning and leasing an asset, the costs would be identical in an efficient capital market. However, due to the different tax treatment as well as the diverse abilities of tax entities to currently utilize the tax benefits associated with ownership, no set rule can be offered as to whether borrowing to buy or a true lease is the cheaper form of financing. Various factors must be analyzed to assess the least costly financing method. A framework for such an analysis is given in Chapter 12.

The cost of a true lease depends on the size of the transaction and whether the lease is tax-oriented or non–tax-oriented. The equipment leasing market can be classified into the following three categories: (1) small-ticket retail market with transactions in the $5,000 to $100,000 range, (2) middle market with large-ticket items covering transactions between $100,000 and $5 million, and (3) special products market involving equipment cost in excess of $5 million.

Tax-oriented leases generally fall into the second and third markets. Most of the leveraged lease transactions are found in the third market and the upper range of the second market. The effective interest cost implied by these lease arrangements is considerably below prevailing interest rates that the same lessee would pay on borrowed funds. Even so, the potential lessee must weigh the lost economic benefits from owning the asset against the economic benefits to be obtained from leasing.

Non–tax-oriented leases fall primarily into the small-ticket retail market and the lower range of the second market. There is no real cost savings associated with these leases compared to traditional borrowing arrangements. In most cases, however, cost is not the dominant motive of the firm that employs this method of financing.

From a tax perspective, leasing has advantages under the following circumstances that lead to a reduction in cost.

1. A company may be in a tax loss carryforward position and consequently be unable to claim tax benefits associated with equipment ownership currently or for several years in the future.

2. A company may be subject to alternative minimum tax and, therefore, be unable to make efficient use of MACRS depreciation deductions.

3. Leasing is ideal for joint venture partnerships in which tax benefits are not available to one or more of the joint venturers because of the way in which the joint venture is structured or because of the particular tax situation of one or more of the joint venture partners. In such cases, the lessor may utilize the tax benefits that would otherwise be wasted and pass those benefits through to the joint venturers in the form of lower lease payments.

4. Leasing also works well for project financings structured through subsidiaries not consolidated for tax purposes and, consequently, not usually in a position to claim and use tax benefits from equipment acquisitions.

5. A company with foreign tax credits may find it difficult to claim tax deductions and any available tax credits under the tax formula for claiming the foreign tax credit.

6. Where costs of plant and equipment expected to be financed by tax-free industrial revenue bonds exceed statutory limits, equipment can often be acquired through a lease to keep the remainder of the project within the bond limits. This is very important in preserving the tax-free characteristics of the bonds.

Sale-and-Leasebacks to Lock in Deferred Tax

Companies concerned that tax rates may rise in the future may wish to do a *sale-and-leaseback* of property that is subject to a large deferred income tax liability resulting from prior accelerated depreciation deductions, in order to "lock in" the future deferred taxes at the current tax rate. The lease rate may, of course, reflect the lessor's view as to possible tax rate changes in the future. If the lessee were to indemnify the lessor for future tax rate changes, the economics would be less attractive for the lessee.

Conservation of Working Capital

The most frequent advantage cited by leasing company representatives and lessees is that leasing conserves working capital. The reasoning is as follows: When a firm borrows money to purchase equipment, the lending institution very rarely provides an amount equal to the entire price of the asset to be financed. Instead, the lender requires the borrowing firm to take an equity position in the asset by making a down payment.[3] The amount of the down payment will depend on such factors as the type of asset, the credit worthiness

---

[3] The Internal Revenue Service does not permit an investment by the lessee in any event.

of the borrower, and prevailing economic conditions. Leasing, on the other hand, typically provides 100% financing since it does not require the firm to make a down payment. Moreover, costs incurred to acquire the equipment, such as delivery and installation charges, are not usually covered by a loan agreement. They may, however, be structured into a lease agreement.

The validity of this argument for financially sound firms during normal economic conditions is questionable. Such firms can simply obtain a loan for 100% of the equipment or borrow the down payment from another source that provides unsecured credit. On the other hand, there is doubt that the funds needed by a small firm for a down payment can be borrowed, particularly during tight money periods. Also, some leases do, in fact, require a down payment in the form of advance lease payments or security deposits at the beginning of the lease term.

Preservation of Credit Capacity by Avoiding Capitalization

Prior to 1973 financial reporting standards did not mandate the disclosure of lease obligations. Thus, leasing was commonly referred to as *off-balance sheet financing*. Current financial reporting standards for leases require that lease obligations classified as capital leases be capitalized as a liability on the balance sheet. According to FASB Statement No. 13, the principle for classifying a lease as a capital lease for financial reporting purposes is as follows:

> A lease that transfers substantially all of the benefits and risks incident to ownership of property should be accounted for as the acquisition of an asset and the incurrence of an obligation by the lessee.

FASB Statement No. 13 specifies four criteria for classifying a lease as a capital lease. Leases not classified as capital leases are considered operating leases. Unlike a capital lease, an operating lease is not capitalized. Instead, certain information regarding such leases must be disclosed in a footnote to the financial statement.

Many chief financial officers are of the opinion that avoiding capitalization of a lease will enhance the financial image of their corporations. Since there is generally ample room for designing lease arrangements so as to avoid having a lease classified as a capital lease, CFOs generally prefer that lease agreements be structured as operating leases.

As a practical matter, in the experience of the authors, 80% to 90% of all long-term true leases (payout type leases for the lessors) are structured to qualify as operating leases for financial accounting purposes for the lessees at the request of the lessees.

Risk of Obsolescence and Disposal of Equipment

When a firm owns equipment, it faces the possibility that at some future time the asset may not be as efficient as more recently manufactured equipment. The owner may then elect to sell the original equipment and purchase the newer, more technologically efficient version. The sale of the equipment, however, may produce only a small fraction of its book value. By leasing, it is argued, the firm may avoid the risk of obsolescence and the problems of asset disposal. The validity of this argument depends on the type of lease and the provisions therein.

With a cancelable operating lease, the lessee can avoid the risk of obsolescence by terminating the contract. However, the avoidance of risk is not without a cost since the rental under such lease arrangements reflects the risk of obsolescence perceived by the lessor.[4] At the end of the lease term, the disposal of the obsolete equipment becomes the problem of the lessor. The risk of loss in residual value that the lessee passes on to the lessor is embodied in the cost of the lease.

The risk of disposal faced by some lessors, however, may not be as great as the risk that would be encountered by the lessee. Some lessors, for example, specialize in short-term operating leases of particular types of equipment, such as, computers or construction

---

[4] Some full payout leases also provide for early termination should the leased property become obsolete to the lessee's needs. However, the lessee in a full payout lease is then liable for a termination payment which reflects the difference between the then value of the equipment and the lessor's uncovered investment, costs, and contemplated profit on the transaction.

equipment, and have the expertise to release or sell equipment coming off lease with substantial remaining useful life. A manufacturer-lessor has less investment exposure since its manufacturing costs will be significantly less than the retail price. Also, it is often equipped to handle reconditioning and redesigning due to technological improvements. Moreover, the manufacturer-lessor will be more active in the resale market for the equipment and thus be in a better position to find users for equipment that may be obsolete to one firm but still satisfactory to another. This reduced risk of disposal, compared with that faced by the lessee, is presumably passed along to the lessee in the form of a reduced lease cost.

Restrictions on Management

When a lender provides funds to a firm for an extended period of time, provisions to protect the lender are included in the debt contract. The purpose of protective provisions, or protective covenants, is to ensure that the borrower remains creditworthy during the period over which the funds are borrowed. Protective provisions impose restrictions on the borrower. Failure to satisfy such a protective covenant usually creates an event of default that, if not cured upon notice, gives the lenders certain additional rights and remedies under the loan agreement, including the right to perfect a security agreement or to demand the immediate repayment of the principal. In practice, the remedy and ability to cure vary with the seriousness of the event of default.

Three general types of protective provisions are imposed by lenders regardless of whether the funds borrowed are provided by a financial institution, such as a bank or life insurance company, or via a bond issue. One type of protective provision seeks to safeguard the liquidity of the borrower.

Routine provisions are a second type of protective covenant. These provisions include such requirements as providing periodic financial statements, restrictions on the sale or pledging of assets, and payment of other obligations. Most important for our discussion is the inclusion of a provision that prohibits the borrower from circumventing the restriction on indebtedness and capital expenditures by leasing. A limit may be imposed on the dollar amount, the term, or the type of leasing obligations.

Finally, specific protective provisions may address particular situations. Examples of such provisions are: specification of how the funds borrowed will be used by the borrower, a management clause that mandates the continued employment of key officers during the borrowing period, and an after-acquired property clause. The last provision specifies that collateral for the borrowed funds is not only that which is indicated in the loan agreement or bond indenture but also includes any similar property acquired by the borrower in the future. Such a provision makes it difficult for the borrower to obtain additional financing, since it prohibits management from using property to be acquired in the future as collateral for a new loan.

An advantage of leasing is that leases typically do not impose financial covenants and restrictions on management as does a loan agreement used to finance the purchase of equipment. The historic reason for this in true leases is that the Internal Revenue Service discouraged true leases from having attributes of loan agreements. Leases may contain restrictions as to location of the property and additional investments by the lessee in the leased equipment in order to ensure compliance with tax laws.

Flexibility and Convenience

In addition to the flexibility and convenience that may result from leasing due to fewer restrictions being imposed on management, five other reasons are often cited for leasing. These reasons are characterized by flexibility and convenience.

Tailor-Made Lease Payments

Lease payment schedules can sometimes be designed to meet the specific needs of the lessee. For example, lease payments can be reduced or not scheduled during the period when the firm has its greatest needs for working capital. Payments can be set higher during the later years of the lease and lower in the earlier years, subject to Internal Revenue requirements, where the lessee's objective is a low present value cost. Although it may be possible to structure a term loan in the same way, it is generally difficult to do so. Moreover, the term for a true lease can usually be structured for a longer period than is customary for conventional loan agreements. Lessors can offer longer terms than bank term loans because of longer-term borrowing to fund activities and faster return of capital as a result of cash flow generated by tax benefits.

Speed in Obtaining Financing

E-commerce leases make a routine lease closing almost instantaneous with the decision to acquire certain types of equipment. A more complex single investor lease can generally be arranged more quickly than financing with other sources of intermediate-term debt. Documentation is usually simpler for closing leasing deals than for other financing arrangements. However, where large-ticket items are financed using a leveraged lease, it may take just as much time, or possibly longer, to put together an acceptable package for all parties as it would take to structure a term loan or arrange a private placement of bonds.

Some lessors write master leases to facilitate quick handling of a series of deliveries of various equipment. A master lease agreement works like a line of credit. Such an arrangement permits the lessee to acquire equipment when needed without having to negotiate a new lease agreement each time equipment is acquired. A restriction is placed on both the dollar amount of equipment to be leased and the time period over which the master lease is to apply. Generally, the time period is less than one year. The interest rate is either agreed to at the outset or is indexed to a reference interest rate at the time of acceptance. As equipment is delivered and accepted by the lessee, the lessee and lessor sign a schedule describing the equipment and lease term that is then incorporated into the master lease agreement by reference. One major advantage to the lessee is that financing costs and conditions of the lease are known in advance. Another advantage is the simple documentation requirements after the master lease agreement is in place.

Regulatory Ease

Public disclosure of financial information and confidential trade information is not required in connection with a lease transaction, as is the case with a prospectus for a public offering of debt or equity and as is sometimes the case with a private offering prospectus or memorandum. Moreover, compliance by the lessee with SEC regulations governing the issuance of securities is not required under a lease. A special financial audit is not usually necessary. Finally, leasing enables companies subject to regulation to avoid obtaining regulatory approval and competitive bidding requirements for financing equipment.

Getting around Budget Limitations

Acquisition of equipment not contemplated by a capital expenditure budget can sometimes be accomplished through use of a lease, with lease payments structured to be classified as an operating expense. This is a common reason for leasing where a company (or a division of a company) has its capital budget in place and desires to acquire equipment to take advantage of a profit opportunity. Rather than go back to the board, the chairman, and so forth, to reopen the budget, the company leases the equipment and reflects it as an expense.

In many firms division managers may be authorized to make current expenditures but not capital expenditures, which are usually reserved to corporate management. Leasing provides a way to circumvent this budgeting restriction for small-ticket items.

Eliminates Maintenance Problems

Of course, for a lease structured as a net lease, maintenance problems are not eliminated but are the responsibility of the lessee. Although an operating lease in which the lessor agrees to maintain the equipment eliminates maintenance problems for the lessee, the cost of maintenance is reflected in the lessor's pricing of the lease. If the lessor under an operating lease is the manufacturer and provides a service contract if the equipment is purchased, the relative unbundled maintenance cost implied in the lease must be compared with the same cost if the equipment is purchased in conjunction with a service contract in order to determine the least expensive operating lease arrangement.

Impact on Cash Flow and Book Earnings

In a properly structured true lease arrangement, the lower lease payment from leasing rather than borrowing can provide a lessee with a superior cash flow. Whether the cash flow stream on an after-tax basis after taking the residual value of the equipment into account is superior on a present value basis must be ascertained. The analysis of cash flows from leasing versus borrowing to purchase are explained in Chapter 12.

Lease payments under a true lease will usually have less impact on book earnings during the early years of the lease than will depreciation and interest payments associated with the purchase of the same equipment.

LEASE BROKERS AND FINANCIAL ADVISERS

The growth of the leasing industry has produced a demand for intermediaries to assist lessors in servicing lessees. Lease brokers and financial advisers serve as architects or packagers of lease transactions by bringing together lessors, lessees, and, in the case of a leveraged lease, third-party lenders. Leasing subsidiaries of banks and bank holding companies, investment bankers, commercial banks, and small independent leasing companies have all played an important role as lease brokers and financial advisers.

Lease brokers and financial advisers can perform a useful service for both lessees and lessors in arranging equipment leases. They can be especially helpful to a lessee by obtaining attractive pricing from a legitimate investor and advising the lessee in structuring and negotiating the transaction. While lease brokers and financial advisers typically represent lessees, they can be helpful to a lessor in finding solutions to negotiating issues.

The services performed by skilled brokers and financial advisers represent real value-added services that result in lower costs for lessees.

For its services as an intermediary, the lease broker or financial adviser receives a brokerage commission. The amount of the remuneration can vary widely, depending on the complexity of the deal and the attractiveness of the deal to the lessor in the prevailing economic environment. The standard fee usually ranges from ½% to 4% of the cost of the equipment, depending on the services performed or provided by the broker and the size and difficulty of the transaction. In some brokered transactions, the lease broker or financial adviser may also receive at least a portion of its compensation in the form of a share participation in the residual value of the leased equipment. And in still other situations the broker or financial adviser will work for a flat fee.

In some instances a broker may assume some equipment risk by purchasing equipment on speculation: the equipment can be leased (or sold) at a later date. Where a broker assumes such equipment risks, the rewards can be substantial. For example, suppose a lease broker purchases an asset such as an executive jet aircraft that requires a two-year lead time for delivery. When the airplane is delivered its market value may be greater than the purchase price paid by the lease broker two years earlier. The lease broker will then line up a lessee (who needs the services of the airplane but cannot wait two years for delivery) and a lessor interested in a tax-sheltered lease. The lease broker then assigns its purchase contract for the aircraft to the lessor and structures the lease payments so that the latter receives the necessary after-tax rate of return necessary to make the deal attractive. The lease broker's compensation in this transaction will consist of two parts: (1) a brokerage fee and (2) profit realized from the sale of its purchase contract. Of course, the lease broker in its position as an equipment speculator may realize a loss rather than a profit. Needless to say, speculation on future values of equipment such as aircraft is risky.

SELECTING A LESSOR OR FINANCIAL ADVISER TO ARRANGE A LEASE

Because of the low entry cost and easy access by lessors into the leasing industry, the potential lessee should exert caution in selecting a lessor, lease broker, or financial adviser. Negotiating a lease with a lessor or lease broker who is incapable of satisfying the lessee's objectives wastes management's time and delays the acquisition of the asset the firm seeks to lease. Moreover, even if a deal is consummated, the lease terms may fail to satisfy a tax and/or financial accounting result sought by the lessee.

Some lessors and lease brokers or packagers tend to quote unrealistically low lease rates only to request a renegotiation at a later time. The low lease rate may not always be a ploy to deceive the potential lessee. Sometimes it may simply be due to a lessor's or packager's belief that a deal can be put together on favorable terms, but subsequent changes in economic or market conditions may make the initial goal impossible.

The lessee should have a feel for prevailing lease rates. In the highly competitive leasing industry, the lease rates quoted should not vary significantly among lessors and packagers.

The dollar size of the transaction and the type of equipment will influence the selection of a lessor or lease broker. Lessors or lease brokers generally establish minimum dollar amounts for transactions they are willing to consider. Lessors will usually go below their minimum target in order to foster a relationship with a new client who may generate more financing activity in the future.

Companies may wish to employ lease financing for equipment to be used in operations by overseas subsidiaries. Because legal and tax aspects of lease transactions differ in every country, most lessors or financial advisors do not have the skills to engage in international or cross-border leasing.[5] Some of the larger commercial banks with international branches do have expertise in writing international leases and some very able independent brokers specialize in these transactions.

A lessee, however, need not rely solely on a U.S. lessor when seeking to lease equipment that will be used in a foreign country. Foreign banks and leasing companies throughout the world provide equipment lease financing. To facilitate the introduction of lessees in one country to lessors in another country, several international equipment lease clubs have been formed with varied effectiveness.

Exhibit 1 lists questions that a potential lessee should consider before selecting a leasing company.

LEASE PROGRAMS

Lessors can structure lease transactions to suit the needs of most companies. Examples of various lease programs available are described below.

---

[5] A lease agreement that establishes the rights of a lessor in one country, for example, may imperil them in another.

Exhibit 1: Evaluating a Lessor, Broker, or Financial Adviser

In evaluating the choice of a lessor, broker, or financial adviser, a lessee should ask the following questions regarding the firms being considered. Every "no" answer regarding a prospective lessor, broker, or financial adviser should make the lessee apprehensive regarding the capacity of that lessor, broker, or financial adviser to perform as represented and in a manner satisfactory to the lessee. Furthermore, the degree of risk rises with the number of "no" answers.

	Yes	No
1. If the firm is a lessor, rather than a broker, will sign a firm commitment subject only to documentation.		
2. Will not broker the transaction to a third party who will be unreasonable to deal with. If problems develop with the proposed investor the broker will locate another investor at no additional cost.		
3. Is adequately capitalized to back up any firm commitment.		
4. Will furnish an audited statement; will state net worth.		
5. Is substantial from a financial and management point of view.		
6. Is experienced and has a clear history in the equipment leasing business. Has a good track record.		
7. Has a good anticipated future in equipment leasing and will be available for consultation throughout the term of the lease.		
8. Is not a promoter type who will disappear after payment of his fee.		
9. Is familiar with the special legal problems related to a lease.		
10. Understands and can correctly analyze the income tax considerations.		
11. Will disclose the full amount of any fees he will receive in the transaction.		
12. The "leasing company" has not purposely submitted a "low-ball" bid.		
13. All material facts will be presented in obtaining any needed tax ruling since the ruling may be valueless if this is not the case, and the lessee may then be liable under the tax indemnity clause.		
14. The transaction may be booked for financial accounting purposes as presented.		
15. If a lessor, has sufficient financial resources to do follow-on lease financing of retrofits, improvements, or additions.		
16. Will not broker the lease to a syndicate of parties, not one of whom can bind the others and who will be difficult to deal with as a group if changes are later needed.		
17. Will not disrupt the lessee's credit standing by indiscriminately contacting financial debt and credit sources all over the country in attempting to broker the transaction.		
18. If the commitment is not firm, the broker or financial adviser will disclose in advance how he will go about finding equity participants and whom he will contact.		
19. If the broker or financial adviser intends to bring in other brokers to help find equity participants, he will disclose who they are, whom they will contact, the amount of their fees, and who will pay the fees.		
20. The broker or financial adviser will make correct representations to the equity participants, so that they will thoroughly understand their rights and obligations under the lease and not become disgruntled investors with whom it will be difficult to deal, should the need arise.		
21. The equity participants will be financially able to meet their obligations to the owner trustee.		
22. The services to be performed by the broker or financial adviser represent real value-added services that result in a lower overall cost for the lessee than the lessee could achieve by dealing directly with a lessor. This is the most important test.		

A standard lease provides 100% long-term financing with level payments over the term of the lease. Standard documentation facilitates quick handling and closing of the lease transaction. Installation costs, delivery charges, transportation expense, and taxes applicable to the purchase of the equipment may be included as part of the lease financing package.

A custom lease contains special provisions designed to meet particular needs of a lessee. It may, for example, schedule lease payments to fit cash flow. Such a lease can be particularly helpful to a seasonal business.

A master lease, as discussed earlier, works like a line of credit. It is an agreement that allows the lessee to acquire during a fixed period of time assets as needed without having to renegotiate a new lease contract for each item. With this arrangement, the lessee and lessor agree to the fixed terms and conditions that will apply for various classifications of equipment for a specified period, usually six months to one year. At any time within that period, the lessee can add equipment to the lease up to an agreed maximum, knowing in advance the rate to be paid and the leasing conditions.

Designed as a sales tool for equipment manufacturers or distributors, a vendor lease program permits suppliers to offer financing in the form of true or conditional sale leases. Vendor leases may be structured as tax-oriented or non–tax-oriented leases. They may be either short-term operating leases or full payout leases. Vendor lease programs can be offered directly by manufacturers and distributors or in conjunction with a third-party leasing company.

An offshore lease is an agreement to lease equipment to be used outside the United States. Offshore lease programs offer leases calling for payments to U.S. lessors in U.S. dollars or local currencies for equipment used abroad. Both true leases and conditional sale leases can be arranged for firms requiring capital equipment in overseas operations. However, the tax benefits to U.S. lessors are insignificant since little depreciation is available on equipment located outside of the United States. Offshore leases are one type of cross-border lease.

Sale-and-lease-back transactions can be used by a company to convert owned property and equipment into cash. The asset is purchased by the lessor and then leased back to the seller. (Care must be taken to comply with bulk sales laws and similar provisions of the commercial code. Usury laws should also be reviewed and sales tax consequences should be understood.)

Under a facility lease, an entire facility—a plant and its equipment—can be leased. Under this arrangement a lessor may provide or arrange construction financing for a facility. Interest costs during construction can often be capitalized into the lease. The lease commences when the completed facility has been accepted by the lessee.

Lease agreements designed for specific assets are sometimes referred to by a description of their generic equipment. For example, computer leases permitting additions of memory core, upgrades, and special features during the course of the initial lease can be arranged. Ship leases utilizing a leveraged lease and Title XI guaranteed debt can be arranged. There are fleet leases for cars and trucks, including TRAC leases containing terminal rental adjustment clauses.

LEVERAGED LEASE FUNDAMENTALS

The leveraged form of a true lease of equipment is the ultimate form of lease financing. The most attractive feature of a leveraged lease, from the standpoint of a lessee unable to use tax benefits of MACRS, is its low cost as compared to that of alternative methods of financing. Leveraged leasing also satisfies a need for lease financing of especially large capital equipment projects with economic lives of up to 25 or more years, although leveraged leases are also used where the life of the equipment is considerably shorter. The leveraged lease can be a most advantageous financing device when used for the right kinds of projects and structured correctly.

Single-investor nonleveraged leases of equipment are simple two-party transactions involving a lessee and a lessor. In single-investor leases, the lessor provides all of the funds necessary to purchase the leased asset from its own resources. While the lessor may borrow some or all of these funds, it does so on a full-recourse basis to its lenders, and it is at risk for all of the capital employed.

A leveraged lease of equipment is conceptually similar to a single-investor lease. The lessee selects the equipment and negotiates the lease in much the same manner. Also, the terms for rentals, options, and responsibility for taxes, insurance, and maintenance are similar. However, a leveraged lease is appreciably more complex in size, documentation, legal involvement, and, most importantly, the number of parties involved and the unique advantages that each party gains.

The lessor in a leveraged lease of equipment becomes the owner of the leased equipment by providing only a percentage (20%–30%) of the capital necessary to purchase the equipment. The remainder of the capital (70%–80%) is borrowed from institutional investors on a nonrecourse basis to the lessor. This loan is secured by a first lien on the equipment, an assignment of the lease, and an assignment of the lease rental payments. The cost of the nonrecourse borrowing is a function of the credit standing of the lessee. The lease rate varies with the debt rate and with the risk of the transaction.

A "leveraged lease" is always a true lease. The lessor in a leveraged lease can claim all of the tax benefits incidental to ownership of the leased asset even though the lessor provides only 20% to 30% of the capital needed to purchase the equipment. This ability to claim the MACRS tax benefits attributable to the entire cost of the leased equipment and the right to 100% of the residual value provided by the lease, while providing and being at risk for only a portion of the cost of the leased equipment, is the "leverage" in a leveraged lease. This leverage enables the lessor in a leveraged lease to offer the lessee much lower lease rates than the lessor could provide under a direct lease.

The legal expenses and closing costs associated with leveraged leases are larger than those for single-investor nonleveraged leases and usually confine the use of leveraged leases to financing relatively large capital equipment acquisitions. However, leveraged leases are also used for smaller lease transactions that are repetitive in nature and use standardized documentation so as to hold down legal and closing costs.

Several parties may be involved in a leveraged lease. Direct or single-investor nonleveraged leases are basically two-party transactions with a lessee and a lessor. However, leveraged leases by their nature involve a minimum of three parties with diverse interests: a lessee, a lessor, and a nonrecourse lender. Indeed, leveraged leases are sometimes called *three-party transactions*.

Several owners and lenders may be involved in a large leveraged lease. In such a case, an owner trustee is generally named to hold title to the equipment and represent the owners or equity participants, and an indenture trustee is usually named to hold the security interest or mortgage on the property for the benefit of the lenders or loan participants. Sometimes a single trustee may be appointed to perform both of these functions.

Structure of a Leveraged Lease

A leveraged lease transaction is usually structured as follows where a broker or a third-party leasing company arranges the transaction.

The leasing company arranging the lease, "the packager," enters into a commitment letter with the prospective lessee (obtains a mandate) that outlines the terms for the lease of the equipment, including the timing and amount of rental payments. Since the exact rental payment cannot be determined until the debt has been sold and the equipment delivered, rents are agreed upon based on certain variables, including assumed debt rates and the delivery dates of the equipment to be leased.

After the commitment letter has been signed, the packager prepares a summary of terms for the proposed lease and contacts potential equity participants to arrange for firm commitments to invest equity in the proposed lease to the extent that the packager does not intend to provide the total amount of the required equity funds from its own resources. Contacts with potential equity sources may be fairly informal or may be accomplished through a bidding process. Typical equity participants include banks, independent finance companies, captive finance companies, and corporate investors that have tax liability to shelter, have funds to invest, and understand the economics of tax-oriented leasing. The packager may also arrange the debt either directly or in conjunction with the capital markets group of a bank or an investment banker selected by the lessee or the lessor. If the equipment is not to be delivered and the lease is not to commence for a considerable period of time, the debt arrangements may be deferred until close to the date of delivery.

The packager may agree at the outset to "bid firm" or underwrite the transaction on the mandated terms and may then "syndicate" its bid to potential equity participants. However, the lessee may prefer to use a bidding procedure without an underwritten price on the theory that more favorable terms can be arranged using this approach.

In some instances the lessee may prefer to prepare its own bid request and solicit bids directly from potential lessors without using a packager or broker to underwrite or arrange the transaction. This might be the case, for example, where the lessee has considerable experience in leveraged leasing and the transaction is repetitious of previous leases of similar equipment that the lessee has leased, such as computers or computer systems.

If an owner trustee is to be used, a bank or trust company mutually agreeable to the equity participants and the lessee is selected to act as owner trustee. If an indenture trustee is to be used, another bank or trust company acceptable to the loan participants is selected to act as indenture trustee. As discussed previously, a single trustee may act as both owner trustee and indenture trustee.

Exhibit 2 illustrates the parties, cash flows, and agreements among the parties in a simple leveraged lease.

If the leveraged lease is arranged by sponsors of a project who want to be the equity participants, the structure and procedures are essentially the same as those for a leveraged lease by a third-party equity participant. In such circumstances, the sponsors are the equity investors. If some of the sponsors can use tax benefits and some cannot, the equity participants may include a combination of sponsors and one or more third-party leasing companies. This arrangement is more complex, but the structure and procedures are essentially the same as those for a leveraged lease by a third-party equity participant.

Key Documents

The key document in a leveraged lease transaction is the participation agreement (sometimes called the *financing agreement*). This document is, in effect, a script for closing the transaction.

Exhibit 2: Leveraged Lease

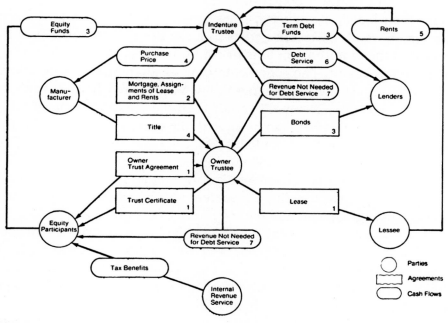

Summary:

1. An owner trust is established by the equity participants, trust certificates are issued, and a lease agreement is signed by the owner trustee as lessor and the lessee.

2. A security agreement is signed by the owner trustee and the indenture trustee, a mortgage is granted on the leased asset, and the lease and rentals are assigned as security to the indenture trustee.

3. Notes or bonds are issued by the owner trustee to the lenders, term debt funds are paid by the lenders (loan participants) to the indenture trustee, and equity funds are paid by the equity participants to the indenture trustee.

4. The purchase price is paid, and title is assigned to the owner trustee, subject to the mortgage.

5. The lease commences; rents are paid by the lessee to the indenture trustee.

6. Debt service is paid by the indenture trustee to the lenders (loan participants).

7. Revenue not required for debt service or trustees' fees is paid to the owner trustee and, in turn, to the equity participants.

When the parties to a leveraged lease transaction are identified, all of them except the indenture trustee enter into a participation agreement that spells out in detail the various undertakings, obligations, mechanics, timing, conditions precedent, and responsibilities of the parties with respect to providing funds and purchasing, leasing, and securing or mortgaging the equipment to be leased.

More specifically: The equity participants agree to provide their investment or equity contribution; the loan participants agree to make their loans; the owner trustee agrees to purchase and lease the equipment; and the lessee agrees to lease the equipment. The substance of the required opinions of counsel is described in the participation agreement. The representations of the parties are detailed. Tax indemnities and other general indemnities are often set forth in the participation agreement rather than the lease agreement. The exact form of agreements to be signed, the opinions to be given, and the representations to be made by the parties are usually attached as exhibits to the participation agreement.

The other key documents in a leveraged lease transaction in addition to the participation agreement are the lease agreement, the owner trust agreement, and the indenture trust agreement.

The lease agreement is between the lessee and owner trustee. The lease is for a term of years and may contain renewal options and fair-market-value purchase options. Rents and all payments due under the lease are net to the lessor, and the lessee waives defenses and offsets to rents under a "hell-or-high-water clause."

The owner trust agreement creates the owner trust and sets forth the relationships between the owner trustee and the equity participants that it represents. The owner trust agreement spells out the duties of the trustee, the documents the trustee is to execute, the distribution to be made of funds it receives from equity participants, lenders, and the lessee. The owner trustee has little or no authority to take discretionary or independent action.

Index

Lightning Source UK Ltd.
Milton Keynes UK
UKOW041055200613

212549UK00001B/1/P